SING FOR JOY IN THE LORD, O YOU RIGHTEOUS ONES

SING FOR JOY
IN THE LORD, O YOU
RIGHTEOUS ONES

Compiled by Eugene Carvalho

Sing for Joy in the Lord, O You Righteous Ones

Copyright © 2020 by Eugene Carvalho

ISBN: 9798594936300

Printed in the United States of America

To the Body of Christ.
May this compilation bless you richly!
With love…

TABLE OF CONTENTS

PURPOSE AND ACKNOWLEDGEMENTS

The infallible Word of God for faith and conduct informs us that the Holy Spirit gives gifts to men and women of the Body of Christ. It states: "the gifts edify the body for the building up of the saints" (Eph. 4:12). I hope the talents and gifts the Lord has given me will be a blessing to someone else through the reading of this compilation.

I am grateful for the love from all family members, especially my wife Mercedes Carvalho. I am also grateful for the knowledge, wisdom and love of many pastors, teachers, and saints that the Lord has used to bless me over the years.

SING FOR JOY IN THE LORD, O YOU RIGHTEOUS ONES

The Bible says, "But about midnight Paul and Silas were praying and singing hymns of praise to God, and the prisoners were listening to them; and suddenly there came a great earthquake, so that the foundations of the prison house were shaken; and immediately all the doors were opened and everyone's chains were unfastened" (Ac. 16:25-26). Singing is powerful.

The writers of the Bible also had much to say regarding joy. Joy is needed living busy lives in a world that is very much out of control. Nehemiah wrote, "Go, eat of the fat, drink of the sweet, and send portions to him who has nothing prepared; for this day is holy to our Lord. Do not be grieved, for the joy of the Lord is your strength" (Ne. 8:10).[1] King David, the mighty warrior, informed us, "For His anger is but for a moment, His favor is for a lifetime; weeping may last for the night, but a shout of joy comes in the morning" (Ps. 30:5).

"The joy that the people of God should have is holy and pure. This joy rises above circumstances and focuses on the very character of God. For example, the psalmist rejoices over God's righteousness (71;14-16), salvation (21:1; 71:23),

---

[1] All Scripture quotations, unless otherwise noted, are from the *New American Standard Bible.*

mercy (31:7), creation (148:5), word (119:4, 162), and faithfulness (33:1-6). God's characteristics as well as His acts are the cause of rejoicing.

"Joy is required of the righteous person (Ps. 150; Phil. 4:4) is produced by the Spirit of God (Gal. 5:22). This kind of joy looks beyond the present to our future salvation (Rom. 5:2; 8:18; 1 Pet. 1:4, 6) and to our sovereign God, who works out all things for our ultimate good, which is Christlikeness (Rom. 8:28-30). This kind of joy is distinct from mere happiness. Joy like this is possible, even in the midst of sorrow (1 Cor. 12:26; 2 Cor. 6:10; 7:4).[2]

Joy is a fruit of the Spirit. "The central passage when discussing spiritual fruit is Galatians 5:22-23, which speaks of the fruit (*karpos*) of the Spirit and then gives a suggested list of nine. The expression 'fruit of the Spirit' is best understood to mean that the Holy Spirit is the source of the fruit. All Christians are required to demonstrate all the fruit of the Spirit. But God does not require all Christians to have all the gifts. It is especially significant that Jesus, in His last discourse, spoke at length about fruit."[3]

With that being said, let's examine a vast array of scriptures that discuss sing, joy, and the righteous. They will give your fresh revelation, build your faith, renew your mind, and bless you.

---

[2] Thomas Nelson, *Nelson's New Illustrated Bible Dictionary* (Nashville: Thomas Nelson Publishers, 1995), p. 709.
[3] Anthony D. Palma, *The Holy Spirit: A Pentecostal Perspective* (Springfield: Logion Press2001), 255.

Chapter Two

SING IN THE OLD TESTAMENT

IN THE BOOK OF EXODUS

I Will Sing, To the Lord, for He is Highly Exalted

"Then Moses and the sons of Israel sang this song to the Lord, and said, 'I will sing to the Lord, for He is highly exalted; The horse and its rider He has hurled into the sea. The Lord is my strength and song, and He has become my salvation; this is my God, and I will praise Him; my father's God, and I will extol Him. The Lord is a warrior; the Lord is His name. Pharaoh's chariots and his army He has cast into the sea; and the choicest of his officers are drowned in the Red Sea. The deeps cover them; they went down into the depths like a stone. Your right hand, O Lord, is majestic in power, Your right hand, O Lord, shatters the enemy. And in the greatness of Your excellence You overthrow those who rise up against You; You send forth Your burning anger, and it consumes them as chaff. At the blast of Your nostrils the waters were piled up, the flowing waters stood up like a heap; the deeps were congealed in the heart of the sea. The enemy said, 'I will pursue, I will overtake, I will divide the spoil; my desire shall be gratified against them; I will draw out my sword, my hand will destroy them.' You blew with Your wind, the sea covered them; they sank like lead in the mighty waters. Who is like You among the gods, O Lord?

Who is like You, majestic in holiness, awesome in praises, working wonders? You stretched out Your right hand, the earth swallowed them. In Your lovingkindness You have led the people whom You have redeemed; in Your strength You have guided them to Your holy habitation. The peoples have heard, they tremble; anguish has gripped the inhabitants of Philistia. Then the chiefs of Edom were dismayed; the leaders of Moab, trembling grips them; all the inhabitants of Canaan have melted away. Terror and dread fall upon them; by the greatness of Your arm they are motionless as stone; until Your people pass over, O Lord, until the people pass over whom You have purchased. You will bring them and plant them in the mountain of Your inheritance, the place, O Lord, which You have made for Your dwelling, the sanctuary, O Lord, which Your hands have established. The Lord shall reign forever and ever" (Ex. 15:1-18)

IN THE BOOK OF NUMBERS

Then Israel Sang This Song: "Spring up, O Well!" Sing to It!

"Then Israel sang this song: 'Spring up, O well! Sing to it! The well, which the leaders sank, which the nobles of the people dug, with the scepter and with their staffs.' And from the wilderness they continued to Mattanah, and from Mattanah to Nahaliel, and from Nahaliel to

Bamoth, and from Bamoth to the valley that is in the land of Moab, at the top of Pisgah which overlooks the wasteland" (Nu. 21:17-20).

IN THE BOOK OF JUDGES

I will Sing Praise to the Lord, the God of Israel

"Then Deborah and Barak the son of Abinoam sang on that day, saying, 'That the leaders led in Israel, that the people volunteered, bless the Lord! Hear, O kings; give ear, O rulers! I—to the Lord, I will sing, I will sing praise to the Lord, the God of Israel. Lord, when You went out from Seir, when You marched from the field of Edom, the earth quaked, the heavens also dripped, even the clouds dripped water. The mountains quaked at the presence of the Lord, this Sinai, at the presence of the Lord, the God of Israel" (Jud. 5:1-5).

You Who Travel on the Road—Sing!

"In the days of Shamgar the son of Anath, In the days of Jael, the highways were deserted, and travelers went by roundabout ways. The peasantry ceased, they ceased in Israel, until I, Deborah, arose, until I arose, a mother in Israel. New gods were chosen; then war was in the gates. Not a shield or a spear was seen among forty thousand in Israel. My heart goes out to the commanders of Israel, the volunteers among the people; bless the Lord! You who ride on white donkeys, you who sit on rich carpets, and you who travel on the road—sing! At the sound of those who divide flocks among the watering places, there they shall recount the righteous deeds of the Lord, the righteous deeds for His peasantry in Israel. Then the people of the Lord went down to the gates" (Jud. 5:6-11).

IN THE BOOK OF 1 SAMUEL

Is This Not David, of Whom They Sing in the Dances

"Now the Philistines gathered together all their armies to Aphek, while the Israelites were camping by the spring which is in Jezreel. And the lords of the Philistines were proceeding on by hundreds and by thousands, and David and his men were proceeding on in the rear with Achish. Then the commanders of the Philistines said, 'What are these Hebrews doing here?' And Achish said to the commanders of the Philistines, 'Is this not David, the servant of Saul the king of Israel, who has been with me these days, or rather these years, and I have found no fault in him from the day he deserted to me to this day?' But the commanders of the Philistines were angry with him, and the commanders of the Philistines said to him, 'Make the man go back, that he may return to his place where you have assigned him, and do not let him go down to battle with us, or in the battle he may become an adversary to us. For with what could this man make himself acceptable to his lord? Would it not be with the heads of these men? Is this not David, of whom they sing in the dances, saying, "Saul has slain his thousands, And David his ten thousands"'" (1Sa. 29:1-5)?

IN THE BOOK OF 2 SAMUEL

I Will Sing Praises to Your Name

"Therefore I will give thanks to You, O Lord, among the nations, and I will sing praises to Your name. He is a tower of deliverance to His king, and shows lovingkindness to His anointed, to David and his descendants forever" (2Sa. 22:50-51).

IN THE BOOK OF 1 CHRONICLES

Sing Praises to Him; Speak of All His Wonders

"Then on that day David first assigned Asaph and his relatives to give thanks to the Lord. Oh give thanks to the Lord, call upon His name; make known His deeds among the peoples. Sing to Him, sing praises to Him; speak of all His wonders. Glory in His holy name; let the heart of those who seek the Lord be glad. Seek the Lord and His strength; seek His face continually. Remember His wonderful deeds which He has done, His marvels and the judgments from His mouth, O seed of Israel His servant, sons of Jacob, His chosen ones! He is the Lord our God; His judgments are in all the earth. Remember His covenant forever, the word which He commanded to a thousand generations, the covenant which He made with Abraham, and His oath to Isaac. He also confirmed it to Jacob for a statute, to Israel as an everlasting covenant, saying, 'To you I will give the land of Canaan, as the portion of your inheritance.' When they were only a few in number, very few, and strangers in it, and they wandered about from nation to nation, and from one kingdom to another people, He permitted no man to oppress them, and He reproved kings for their sakes, saying, 'Do not touch My anointed ones, and do My prophets no harm.' Sing to the Lord, all the earth; proclaim good tidings of His salvation from day to day. Tell of His glory among the nations, His wonderful deeds among all the peoples. For great is the Lord, and greatly to be praised; He also is to be feared above all gods. For all the gods of the peoples are idols, but the Lord made the heavens. Splendor and majesty are before Him, strength and joy are in His place. Ascribe to the Lord, O families of the peoples, ascribe to the Lord glory and strength. Ascribe to the Lord the glory due His name; bring an offering, and come before Him; worship the Lord in holy array. Tremble before Him, all the earth; indeed, the world is firmly established, it will not be moved. Let the heavens be glad, and let the earth rejoice; and let them say among the nations,

'The Lord reigns.' Let the sea roar, and all it contains; let the field exult, and all that is in it. Then the trees of the forest will sing for joy before the Lord; for He is coming to judge the earth. O give thanks to the Lord, for He is good; for His lovingkindness is everlasting. Then say, 'Save us, O God of our salvation, and gather us and deliver us from the nations, to give thanks to Your holy name, and glory in Your praise.' Blessed be the Lord, the God of Israel, from everlasting even to everlasting. Then all the people said, 'Amen,' and praised the Lord" (1Ch. 16:7-36).

All These Were Under the Direction of Their Father to Sing in the House of the Lord

"Moreover, David and the commanders of the army set apart for the service some of the sons of Asaph and of Heman and of Jeduthun, who were to prophesy with lyres, harps and cymbals; and the number of those who performed their service was: of the sons of Asaph: Zaccur, Joseph, Nethaniah and Asharelah; the sons of Asaph were under the direction of Asaph, who prophesied under the direction of the king. Of Jeduthun, the sons of Jeduthun: Gedaliah, Zeri, Jeshaiah, Shimei, Hashabiah and Mattithiah, six, under the direction of their father Jeduthun with the harp, who prophesied in giving thanks and praising the Lord. Of Heman, the sons of Heman: Bukkiah, Mattaniah, Uzziel, Shebuel and Jerimoth, Hananiah, Hanani, Eliathah, Giddalti and

Romamti-ezer, Joshbekashah, Mallothi, Hothir, Mahazioth. All these were the sons of Heman the king's seer to exalt him according to the words of God, for God gave fourteen sons and three daughters to Heman. All these were under the direction of their father to sing in the house of the Lord, with cymbals, harps and lyres, for the service of the house of God. Asaph, Jeduthun and Heman were under the direction of the king. Their number who were trained in singing to the Lord, with their relatives, all who were skillful, was 288. They cast lots for their duties, all alike, the small as well as the great, the teacher as well as the pupil" (1Ch. 25:1-8).

IN THE BOOK OF 2 CHRONICLES

King Hezekiah and the Officials Ordered the Levites to Sing Praises

"Now at the completion of the burnt offerings, the king and all who were present with him bowed down and worshiped. Moreover, King Hezekiah and the officials ordered the Levites to sing praises to the Lord with the words of David and Asaph the seer. So they sang praises with joy, and bowed down and worshiped" (2Ch. 29:29-30).

IN THE BOOK OF JOB

They Sing to the Timbrel and Harp

"Then Job answered, 'Listen carefully to my speech, and let this be your way of consolation. Bear with me that I may speak; then after I have spoken, you may mock. As for me, is my complaint to man? And why should I not be impatient? Look at me, and be astonished, and put your hand over your mouth. Even when I remember, I am disturbed, and horror takes hold of my flesh. Why do the wicked still live, continue on, also become very powerful? Their descendants are established with them in their sight, and their offspring before their eyes, their houses are safe from fear, and the rod of God is not on them. His ox mates without fail; his cow calves and does not abort. They send forth their little ones like the flock, and their children skip about. They sing to the timbrel and harp and rejoice at the sound of the flute. They spend their days in prosperity, and suddenly they go down to Sheol. They say to God, "Depart from us! We do not even desire the knowledge of Your ways. Who is the Almighty, that we should serve Him, and what would we gain if we entreat Him?" Behold, their prosperity is not in their hand; the counsel of the wicked is far from me'" (Job 21:1-16).

Chapter Two

I Made the Widow's Heart Sing for Joy

"And Job again took up his discourse and said, 'Oh that I were as in months gone by, as in the days when God watched over me; when His lamp shone over my head, and by His light I walked through darkness; as I was in the prime of my days, when the friendship of God was over my tent; when the Almighty was yet with me, and my children were around me; when my steps were bathed in butter, and the rock poured out for me streams of oil! When I went out to the gate of the city, when I took my seat in the square, the young men saw me and hid themselves, and the old men arose and stood. The princes stopped talking and put their hands on their mouths; the voice of the nobles was hushed, and their tongue stuck to their palate. For when the ear heard, it called me blessed, and when the eye saw, it gave witness of me, because I delivered the poor who cried for help, and the orphan who had no helper. The blessing of the one ready to perish came upon me, and I made the widow's heart sing for joy. I put on righteousness, and it clothed me; my justice was like a robe and a turban. I was eyes to the blind and feet to the lame. I was a father to the needy, and I investigated the case which I did not know. I broke the jaws of the wicked and snatched the prey from his teeth. Then I thought, "I shall die in my nest, and I shall multiply my days as the sand. My root is spread out to the waters, and dew lies all night on my branch. My glory is ever new with me, and my bow is renewed in my hand'"'" (Job 29:1-20).

He Will Sing to Men

"If there is an angel as mediator for him, one out of a thousand, to remind a man what is right for him, then let him be gracious to him, and say, 'Deliver him from going down to the pit, I have found a ransom'; let his flesh become fresher than in youth, let him return to the days of his youthful vigor; then he will pray to God, and He will accept him, that he may see His face with joy, and He may restore His righteousness to man. He will sing to men and say, 'I have sinned and perverted what is right, and it is not proper for me. He has redeemed my soul from going to the pit, and my life shall see the light'" (Job 33:23-28).

IN THE BOOK OF PSALMS

Let Them Ever Sing for Joy; and May You Shelter Them

"But let all who take refuge in You be glad, let them ever sing for joy; and may You shelter them, that those who love Your name may exult in You. For it is You who blesses the righteous man, O Lord, You surround him with favor as with a shield" (Ps. 5:11-12).

Chapter Two

I Will Sing Praise to the Name of the Lord Most High

"I will give thanks to the Lord according to His righteousness and will sing praise to the name of the Lord Most High" (Ps. 7:17).

I Will be Glad and Exult in You; I Will Sing Praise to Your Name

"I will give thanks to the Lord with all my heart; I will tell of all Your wonders. I will be glad and exult in You; I will sing praise to Your name, O Most High" (Ps. 9:1-2).

Sing Praises to the Lord, Who Dwells in Zion

"Sing praises to the Lord, who dwells in Zion; declare among the peoples His deeds. For He who requires blood remembers them; He does not forget the cry of the afflicted. Be gracious to me, O Lord; see my affliction from those who hate me, You who lift me up from the gates of death, that I may tell of all Your praises, that in the gates of the daughter of Zion I may rejoice in Your salvation. The nations have sunk down in the pit which they have made; in the net which they hid, their own foot has been caught. The Lord has made Himself known; He has executed judgment. In the work of his own hands the wicked is snared" (Ps. 9:11-16).

I Will Sing to the Lord, Because He Has Dealt Bountifully with Me

"But I have trusted in Your lovingkindness; my heart shall rejoice in Your salvation. I will sing to the Lord, because He has dealt bountifully with me" (Ps. 13:5-6).

I Will Sing Praises to Your Name

"The Lord lives, and blessed be my rock; and exalted be the God of my salvation, the God who executes vengeance for me, and subdues peoples under me. He delivers me from my enemies; surely You lift me above those who rise up against me; You rescue me from the violent man. Therefore I will give thanks to You among the nations, O Lord, and I will sing praises to Your name. He gives great deliverance to His king, and shows lovingkindness to His anointed, to David and his descendants forever" (Ps. 18:46-50).

We Will Sing for Joy Over Your Victory

"May He grant you your heart's desire and fulfill all your counsel! We will sing for joy over your victory, and in the name of our God we will set up our banners. May the Lord fulfill all your petitions" (Ps. 20:4-5).

Chapter Two

We Will Sing and Praise Your Power

"O Lord, in Your strength the king will be glad, and in Your salvation how greatly he will rejoice! You have given him his heart's desire, and You have not withheld the request of his lips. For You meet him with the blessings of good things; You set a crown of fine gold on his head. He asked life of You, You gave it to him, length of days forever and ever. His glory is great through Your salvation, splendor and majesty You place upon him. For You make him most blessed forever; You make him joyful with gladness in Your presence. For the king trusts in the Lord, and through the lovingkindness of the Most High he will not be shaken. Your hand will find out all your enemies; Your right hand will find out those who hate you. You will make them as a fiery oven in the time of your anger; the Lord will swallow them up in His wrath, and fire will devour them. Their offspring You will destroy from the earth, and their descendants from among the sons of men. Though they intended evil against You and devised a plot, they will not succeed. For You will make them turn their back; You will aim with Your bowstrings at their faces. Be exalted, O Lord, in Your strength; we will sing and praise Your power" (Ps. 21:1-13).

I Will Sing, Yes, I Will Sing Praises to the Lord

"One thing I have asked from the Lord, that I shall seek: that I may dwell in the house of the Lord all the days of my life, to behold the beauty of the Lord And to meditate in His temple. For in the day of trouble He will conceal me in His tabernacle; in the secret place of His tent He will hide me; He will lift me up on a rock. And now my head will be lifted up above my enemies around me, and I will offer in His tent sacrifices with shouts of joy; I will sing, yes, I will sing praises to the Lord" (Ps. 27:4-6).

Sing Praise to the Lord, You His Godly Ones

"I will extol You, O Lord, for You have lifted me up, and have not let my enemies rejoice over me. O Lord my God, I cried to You for help, and You healed me. O Lord, You have brought up my soul from Sheol; You have kept me alive, that I would not go down to the pit. Sing praise to the Lord, you His godly ones, and give thanks to His holy name. For His anger is but for a moment, His favor is for a lifetime; weeping may last for the night, but a shout of joy comes in the morning" (Ps. 30:1-5).

Sing for Joy in the Lord, O You Righteous Ones

"Sing for joy in the Lord, O you righteous ones; praise is becoming to the upright. Give thanks to the Lord with the lyre; sing praises to Him with a harp of ten strings. Sing to Him a new song; play skillfully with a shout of joy. For the word of the Lord is upright, and all His work is done in faithfulness. He loves righteousness and justice; the earth is full of the lovingkindness of the Lord" (Ps. 33:1-5).

Sing Praises; Sing Praises to our King, Sing Praises

"God has ascended with a shout, the Lord, with the sound of a trumpet. Sing praises to God, sing praises; sing praises to our King, sing praises. For God is the King of all the earth; sing praises with a skillful psalm. God reigns over the nations, God sits on His holy throne. The princes of the people have assembled themselves as the people of the God of Abraham, for the shields of the earth belong to God; He is highly exalted" (Ps. 47:5-9).

My Tongue Will Joyfully Sing of Your Righteousness

"Deliver me from bloodguiltiness, O God, the God of my salvation; then my tongue will joyfully sing of Your righteousness. O Lord, open my lips, that my mouth may declare Your praise. For You do not delight in sacrifice, otherwise I would give it; You are not pleased with burnt offering. The sacrifices of God are a broken spirit; a broken and a contrite heart, O God, You will not despise" (Ps. 51:14-17).

I Will Sing, Yes, I Will Sing Praises

"My heart is steadfast, O God, my heart is steadfast; I will sing, yes, I will sing praises! Awake, my glory! Awake, harp and lyre! I will awaken the dawn. I will give thanks to You, O Lord, among the peoples; I will sing praises to You among the nations. For Your lovingkindness is great to the heavens and Your truth to the clouds. Be exalted above the heavens, O God; let Your glory be above all the earth" (Ps. 57:7-11).

I Shall Sing of Your Strength

"But as for me, I shall sing of Your strength; yes, I shall joyfully sing of Your lovingkindness in the morning, for You have been my stronghold and a refuge in the day of my distress. O my strength, I will sing praises to You; for God is my stronghold, the God who shows me lovingkindness" (Ps. 59:16-17).

So I Will Sing Praise to Your Name Forever

"For You have heard my vows, O God; You have given me the inheritance of those who fear Your name. You will prolong the king's life; his years will be as many generations. He will abide before God forever; appoint lovingkindness and truth that they may preserve him. So I will sing praise to Your name forever, that I may pay my vows day by day" (Ps. 61:5-8).

In the Shadow of Your Wings I Sing for Joy

"When I remember You on my bed, I meditate on You in the night watches, for You have been my help, and in the shadow of Your wings I sing for joy. My soul clings to You; Your right hand upholds me. But those who seek my life to destroy it, will go into the depths of the earth. They will be delivered over to the power of the sword; they will be a prey for foxes. But the king will rejoice in God; everyone who swears by Him will glory, for the mouths of those who speak lies will be stopped" (Ps. 63:6-11).

They Shout for Joy, Yes, They Sing

"You visit the earth and cause it to overflow; You greatly enrich it; the stream of God is full of water; You prepare their grain, for thus You prepare the earth. You water its furrows abundantly, You settle its ridges, You soften it with showers, You bless its growth. You have crowned the year with Your bounty, and Your paths drip with fatness. The pastures of the wilderness drip, and the hills gird themselves with rejoicing. The meadows are clothed with flocks and the valleys are covered with grain; they shout for joy, yes, they sing" (Ps. 65:9-13).

Sing the Glory of His Name; Make His Praise Glorious

"Shout joyfully to God, all the earth; sing the glory of His name; make His praise glorious. Say to God, 'How awesome are Your works! Because of the greatness of Your power Your enemies will give feigned obedience to You. All the earth will worship You, and will sing praises to You; they will sing praises to Your name'" (Ps. 66:1-4).

Let the Nations Be Glad and Sing for Joy

"God be gracious to us and bless us, and cause His face to shine upon us—Selah. That Your way may be known on the earth, Your salvation among all nations. Let the peoples praise You, O God; let all the peoples praise You. Let the nations be glad and sing for joy; for You will judge the peoples with uprightness and guide the nations on the earth. Let the peoples praise You, O God; let all the peoples praise You. The earth has yielded its produce; God, our God, blesses us. God blesses us, that all the ends of the earth may fear Him" (Ps. 67:1-7).

Sing to God, Sing Praises to His Name

"Let God arise, let His enemies be scattered, and let those who hate Him flee before Him. As smoke is driven away, so drive them away; as wax melts before the fire, so let the wicked perish before God. But let the righteous be glad; let them exult before God; Yes, let them rejoice with gladness. Sing to God, sing praises to His name; lift up a song for Him who rides through the deserts, whose name is the Lord, and exult before Him" (Ps. 68:1-4).

Sing to God, O Kingdoms of the Earth, Sing Praises to the Lord

"Sing to God, O kingdoms of the earth, sing praises to the Lord, Selah. To Him who rides upon the highest heavens, which are from ancient times; behold, He speaks forth with His voice, a mighty voice. Ascribe strength to God; His majesty is over Israel and His strength is in the skies. O God, You are awesome from Your sanctuary. The God of Israel Himself gives strength and power to the people. Blessed be God" (Ps. 68:32-35)!

I Will Sing Praises with the Lyre, O Holy One of Israel

"I will also praise You with a harp, even Your truth, O my God; to You I will sing praises with the lyre, O Holy One of Israel. My lips will shout for joy when I sing praises to You; and my soul, which You have redeemed. My tongue also will utter Your righteousness all day long; for they are ashamed, for they are humiliated who seek my hurt" (Ps. 71:22-24).

I Will Sing Praises to the God of Jacob

"For not from the east, nor from the west, nor from the desert comes exaltation; but God is the Judge; He puts down one and exalts another. For a cup is in the hand of the Lord, and the wine foams; it is well mixed, and He pours out of this; surely all the wicked of the earth must drain and drink down its dregs. But as for me, I will declare it forever; I will sing praises to the God of Jacob" (Ps. 75:6-9).

Sing for Joy to God Our Strength

"Sing for joy to God our strength; shout joyfully to the God of Jacob. Raise a song, strike the timbrel, the sweet sounding lyre with the harp. Blow the trumpet at the new moon, at the full moon, on our feast day. For it is a statute for Israel, an ordinance of the God of Jacob. He established it for a testimony in Joseph when he went throughout the land of Egypt. I heard a language that I did not know" (Ps. 81:1-5).

My Heart and My Flesh Sing for Joy to the Living God

"How lovely are Your dwelling places, O Lord of hosts! My soul longed and even yearned for the courts of the Lord; my heart and my flesh sing for joy to the living God. The bird also has found a house, and the swallow a nest for herself, where she may lay her young, even Your altars, O Lord of hosts, My King and my God. How blessed are those who dwell in Your house! They are ever praising You. How blessed is the man whose strength is in You, in whose heart are the highways to Zion! Passing through the valley of Baca they make it a spring; the early rain also covers it with blessings. They go from strength to strength, Every one of them appears before God in Zion" (Ps. 84:1-7).

I Will Sing of the Lovingkindness of the Lord Forever

"I will sing of the lovingkindness of the Lord forever; to all generations I will make known Your faithfulness with my mouth. For I have said, 'Lovingkindness will be built up forever; in the heavens You will establish Your faithfulness.' I have made a covenant with My chosen; I have sworn to David My servant, I will establish your seed forever and build up your throne to all generations" (Ps. 89:1-4).

That We May Sing for Joy and Be Glad All Our Days

"Do return, O Lord; how long will it be? And be sorry for Your servants. O satisfy us in the morning with Your lovingkindness, that we may sing for joy and be glad all our days. Make us glad according to the days You have afflicted us, and the years we have seen evil. Let Your work appear to Your servants and Your majesty to their children. Let the favor of the Lord our God be upon us; and confirm for us the work of our hands; yes, confirm the work of our hands" (Ps. 90:13-17).

Sing Praises to Your Name, O Most High

"It is good to give thanks to the Lord and to sing praises to Your name, O Most High; to declare Your lovingkindness in the morning and Your faithfulness by night, with the ten-stringed lute and with the harp, with resounding music upon the lyre. For You, O Lord, have made me glad by what You have done, I will sing for joy at the works of Your hands" (Ps. 92:1-4).

O Come, Let Us Sing for Joy to the Lord

"O come, let us sing for joy to the Lord, Let us shout joyfully to the rock of our salvation. Let us come before His presence with thanksgiving, let us shout joyfully to Him with psalms. For the Lord is a great God and a great King above all gods, in whose hand are the depths of the earth, the peaks of the mountains are His also. The sea is His, for it was He who made it, and His hands formed the dry land" (Ps. 95:1-5).

Sing to the Lord a New Song; Sing to the Lord, All the Earth

"Sing to the Lord a new song; sing to the Lord, all the earth. Sing to the Lord, bless His name; proclaim good tidings of His salvation from day to day. Tell of His glory among the nations, His wonderful deeds among all the peoples. For great is the Lord and greatly to be praised; He is to be feared above all gods. For all the gods of the peoples are idols, but the Lord made the heavens. Splendor and majesty are before Him, strength and beauty are in His sanctuary" (Ps. 96:1-6).

All the Trees of the Forest Will Sing for Joy

"Let the heavens be glad, and let the earth rejoice; let the sea roar, and all it contains; let the field exult, and all that is in it. Then all the trees of the forest will sing for joy before the Lord, for He is coming, for He is coming to judge the earth. He will judge the world in righteousness and the peoples in His faithfulness" (Ps. 96:11-13).

O Sing to the Lord a New Song, for He Has Done Wonderful Things

"O sing to the Lord a new song, for He has done wonderful things, His right hand and His holy arm have gained the victory for Him. The Lord has made known His salvation; He has revealed His righteousness in the sight of the nations. He has remembered His lovingkindness and His faithfulness to the house of Israel; all the ends of the earth have seen the salvation of our God" (Ps. 98:1-3).

Break Forth and Sing for Joy and Sing Praises

"Shout joyfully to the Lord, all the earth; break forth and sing for joy and sing praises. Sing praises to the Lord with the lyre, with the lyre and the sound of melody. With trumpets and the sound of the horn shout joyfully before the King, the Lord" (Ps. 98:4-6).

Let the Rivers Clap their Hands, Let the Mountains Sing Together for Joy

"Let the sea roar and all it contains, the world and those who dwell in it. Let the rivers clap their hands, let the mountains sing together for joy before the Lord, for He is coming to judge the earth; He will judge the world with righteousness and the peoples with equity" (Ps. 98:7-9).

I Will Sing of Lovingkindness and Justice, To You, O Lord

"I will sing of lovingkindness and justice, To You, O Lord, I will sing praises. I will give heed to the blameless way. When will You come to me? I will walk within my house in the integrity of my heart. I will set no worthless thing before my eyes; I hate the work of those who fall away; it shall not fasten its grip on me. A perverse heart shall depart from me; I will know no evil. Whoever secretly slanders his neighbor, him I will destroy; no one who has a haughty look and an arrogant heart will I endure" (Ps. 101:1-5).

I Will Sing to the Lord as Long as I Live

"Let the glory of the Lord endure forever; let the Lord be glad in His works; He looks at the earth, and it trembles; He touches the mountains, and they smoke. I will sing to the Lord as long as I live; I will sing praise to my God while I have my being. Let my meditation be pleasing to Him; as for me, I shall be glad in the Lord. Let sinners be consumed from the earth and let the wicked be no more. Bless the Lord, O my soul. Praise the Lord" (Ps. 104:31-35)!

Sing to Him, Sing Praises to Him

"Oh give thanks to the Lord, call upon His name; make known His deeds among the peoples. Sing to Him, sing praises to Him; speak of all His wonders. Glory in His holy name; let the heart of those who seek the Lord be glad. Seek the Lord and His strength; seek His face continually. Remember His wonders which He has done, His marvels and the judgments uttered by His mouth, O seed of Abraham, His servant, O sons of Jacob,

His chosen ones! He is the Lord our God; His judgments are in all the earth" (Ps. 105:1-7).

I Will Sing, I Will Sing Praises, Even With My Soul

"My heart is steadfast, O God; I will sing, I will sing praises, even with my soul. Awake, harp and lyre; I will awaken the dawn! I will give thanks to You, O Lord, among the peoples, and I will sing praises to You among the nations. For Your lovingkindness is great above the heavens, and Your truth reaches to the skies. Be exalted, O God, above the heavens, and Your glory above all the earth. That Your beloved may be delivered, save with Your right hand, and answer me" (Ps. 108:1-6)!

Let My Tongue Sing of Your Word

"Let my cry come before You, O Lord; give me understanding according to Your word. Let my supplication come before You; deliver me according to Your word. Let my lips utter praise, for You teach me Your statutes. Let my tongue sing of Your word, for all Your commandments are righteousness. Let Your hand be ready to help me, for I have chosen Your precepts. I long for Your salvation, O Lord, and Your law is my delight. Let my soul live that it may praise You, and let Your ordinances help me. I have gone astray like a lost sheep; seek Your servant, for I do not forget Your commandments" (Ps. 119:169-176).

Let Your Godly Ones Sing for Joy

"Behold, we heard of it in Ephrathah, we found it in the field of Jaar. Let us go into His dwelling place; let us worship at His footstool. Arise, O Lord, to Your resting place, You and the ark of Your strength. Let Your priests be clothed with righteousness, and let Your godly ones sing for joy" (Ps. 132:6-9).

Sing Aloud

"For the Lord has chosen Zion; He has desired it for His habitation. This is My resting place forever; here I will dwell, for I have desired it. I will abundantly bless her provision; I will satisfy her needy with bread. Her priests also I will clothe with salvation, and her godly ones will sing aloud for joy. There I will cause the horn of David to spring forth; I have prepared a lamp for Mine anointed. His enemies I will clothe with shame, but upon himself his crown shall shine" (Ps. 132:13-18).

Sing Praises to His Name, for It Is Lovely

"Praise the Lord! Praise the name of the Lord; praise Him, O servants of the Lord, you who stand in the house of the Lord, in the courts of the house of our God! Praise the Lord, for the Lord is good; sing praises to His name, for it is lovely. For the Lord has chosen Jacob for Himself, Israel for His own possession" (Ps. 135:1-4).

Sing Us One of the Songs of Zion

"By the rivers of Babylon, there we sat down and wept, when we remembered Zion. Upon the willows in the midst of it we hung our harps. For there our captors demanded of us songs, and our tormentors mirth, saying, 'Sing us one of the songs of Zion'" (Ps. 137:1-3).

How Can We Sing the Lord's Song in a Foreign Land?

"How can we sing the Lord's song In a foreign land? If I forget you, O Jerusalem, may my right hand forget her skill. May my tongue cling to the roof of my mouth if I do not remember you, if I do not exalt Jerusalem above my chief joy" (Ps. 137:4-6).

I Will Sing Praises to You Before the Gods

"I will give You thanks with all my heart; I will sing praises to You before the gods. I will bow down toward Your holy temple and give thanks to Your name for Your lovingkindness and Your truth; for You have magnified Your word according to all Your name. On the day I called, You answered me; You made me bold with strength in my soul" (Ps. 138:1-3).

I Will Sing a New Song to You, O God

"I will sing a new song to You, O God; upon a harp of ten strings I will sing praises to You, Who gives salvation to kings, who rescues David His servant from the evil sword. Rescue me and deliver me out of the hand of aliens, whose mouth speaks deceit and whose right hand is a right hand of falsehood" (Ps. 144:9-11).

I Will Sing Praises to My God While I Have My Being

"Praise the Lord! Praise the Lord, O my soul! I will praise the Lord while I live; I will sing praises to my God while I have my being. Do not trust in princes, in mortal man, in whom there is no salvation. His spirit departs, he returns to the earth; in that very day his thoughts perish. How blessed is he whose help is the God of Jacob, whose hope is in the Lord his God, who made heaven and earth, the sea and all that is in them; who keeps faith forever; who executes justice for the oppressed; who gives food to the hungry. The Lord sets the prisoners free" (Ps. 146:1-7).

Sing Praises to Our God; for It Is Pleasant and Praise Is Becoming

"Praise the Lord! For it is good to sing praises to our God; for it is pleasant and praise is becoming. The Lord builds up Jerusalem; He gathers the outcasts of Israel. He heals the brokenhearted and binds up their wounds. He counts the number of the stars; He gives names to all of them. Great is our Lord and abundant in strength; His understanding is infinite. The Lord supports the afflicted; He brings down the wicked to the ground" (Ps. 147:1-6).

Sing to the Lord with Thanksgiving

"Sing to the Lord with thanksgiving; sing praises to our God on the lyre, who covers the heavens with clouds, who provides rain for the earth, who makes grass to grow on the mountains. He gives to the beast its food, and to the young ravens which cry. He does not delight in the strength of the horse; He does not take pleasure in the legs of a man. The Lord favors those who fear Him, those who wait for His lovingkindness" (Ps. 147:7-11).

Sing to the Lord a New Song, and His Praise in the Congregation

"Praise the Lord! Sing to the Lord a new song, and His praise in the congregation of the godly ones. Let Israel be glad in his Maker; let the sons of Zion rejoice in their King. Let them praise His name with dancing; let them sing praises to Him with timbrel and lyre. For the Lord takes pleasure in His people; He will beautify the afflicted ones with salvation" (Ps. 149:1-4).

Let Them Sing for Joy on Their Beds

"Let the godly ones exult in glory; let them sing for joy on their beds. Let the high praises of God be in their mouth, and a two-edged sword in their hand, to execute vengeance on the nations and punishment on the peoples, to bind their kings with chains and their nobles with fetters of iron, to execute on them the judgment written; this is an honor for all His godly ones. Praise the Lord" (Ps. 149:5-9)!

IN THE BOOK OF ECCLESIASTES

All the Daughters of Song Will Sing Softly

"Remember also your Creator in the days of your youth, before the evil days come and the years draw near when you will say, 'I have no delight in them'; before the sun and the light, the moon and the stars are darkened, and clouds return after the rain; in the day that the watchmen of the house tremble, and mighty men stoop, the grinding ones stand idle because they are few, and those who look through windows grow dim; and the doors on the street are shut as the sound of the grinding mill is low, and one will arise at the sound of the bird, and all the daughters of song will sing softly. Furthermore, men are afraid of a high place and of terrors on the road; the almond tree blossoms, the grasshopper drags himself along, and the caperberry is ineffective. For man goes to his eternal home while mourners go about in the street. Remember Him before the silver cord is broken and the golden bowl is crushed, the pitcher by the well is shattered and the wheel at the cistern is crushed; then the dust will return to the earth as it was, and the spirit will return to God who gave it. 'Vanity of vanities,' says the Preacher, 'all is vanity'" (Ec. 12:1-8)!

IN THE BOOK OF ISAIAH

Let Me Sing Now for My Well-Beloved

"Let me sing now for my well-beloved a song of my beloved concerning His vineyard. My well-beloved had a vineyard on a fertile hill. He dug it all around, removed its stones, and planted it with the choicest vine. And He built a tower in the middle of it and also hewed out a wine vat in it; then He expected it to produce good grapes, but it produced only worthless ones" (Is. 5:1-2).

Chapter Two

Sing to the Lord a New Song. Sing His Praise from the End of the Earth

"Sing to the Lord a new song, sing His praise from the end of the earth! You who go down to the sea, and all that is in it. You islands, and those who dwell on them. Let the wilderness and its cities lift up their voices, the settlements where Kedar inhabits. Let the inhabitants of Sela sing aloud, let them shout for joy from the tops of the mountains. Let them give glory to the Lord and declare His praise in the coastlands" (Is. 42:10-12).

IN THE BOOK OF JEREMIAH

Sing to the Lord, Praise the Lord! For He Has Delivered the Soul of the Needy

"O Lord, You have deceived me and I was deceived; You have overcome me and prevailed. I have become a laughingstock all day long; everyone mocks me. For each time I speak, I cry aloud; I proclaim violence and destruction, because for me the word of the Lord has resulted in reproach and derision all day long. But if I say, 'I will not remember Him or speak anymore in His name,' then in my heart it becomes like a burning fire shut up in my bones; and I am weary of holding it in, and I cannot endure it. For I have heard the whispering of many, 'Terror on every side! Denounce him; yes, let us denounce him!' All my trusted friends, watching for my fall, say: 'Perhaps he will be deceived, so that we may prevail against him and take our revenge on him.' But the Lord is with me like a dread champion; therefore my persecutors will stumble and not prevail. They will be utterly ashamed, because they have failed, with an everlasting disgrace that will not be forgotten. Yet, O Lord of hosts, You who test the righteous, who see the mind and the heart; let me see Your vengeance on them; for to You I have set forth my cause. Sing to the Lord, praise the Lord! For He has delivered the soul of the needy one from the hand of evildoers" (Jer. 20:7-13).

Sing Aloud with Gladness for Jacob, and Shout Among the Chief of the Nations

"For thus says the Lord, 'Sing aloud with gladness for Jacob, and shout among the chief of the nations; proclaim, give praise and say, 'O Lord, save Your people, the remnant of Israel.' Behold, I am bringing them from the north country, and I will gather them from the remote parts of the earth, among them the blind and the lame, the woman with child and she who is in labor with child, together; a great company, they will return here. With weeping they will come, and by supplication I will lead them; I will make them walk by streams of waters, on a straight path in which they will not stumble; for I am a father to Israel, and Ephraim is My firstborn" (Jer. 31:7-9).

Chapter Two

IN THE BOOK OF HOSEA

She Will Sing There as in the Days of Her Youth

"Therefore, behold, I will allure her, bring her into the wilderness and speak kindly to her. Then I will give her her vineyards from there, and the valley of Achor as a door of hope. And she will sing there as in the days of her youth, as in the day when she came up from the land of Egypt. 'It will come about in that day,' declares the Lord, 'That you will call Me Ishi And will no longer call Me Baali. For I will remove the names of the Baals from her mouth, so that they will be mentioned by their names no more. In that day I will also make a covenant for them with the beasts of the field, the birds of the sky and the creeping things of the ground. And I will abolish the bow, the sword and war from the land, and will make them lie down in safety. I will betroth you to Me forever; yes, I will betroth you to Me in righteousness and in justice, in lovingkindness and in compassion, and I will betroth you to Me in faithfulness. Then you will know the Lord'" (Hos. 2:14-20).

IN THE BOOK OF ZEPHANIAH

Birds Will Sing in the Window

"'You also, O Ethiopians, will be slain by My sword.' And He will stretch out His hand against the north and destroy Assyria, and He will make Nineveh a desolation, parched like the wilderness. Flocks will lie down in her midst, all beasts which range in herds; both the pelican and the hedgehog will lodge in the tops of her pillars; birds will sing in the window, desolation will be on the threshold; for He has laid bare the cedar work. This is the exultant city which dwells securely, who says in her heart, 'I am, and there is no one besides me.' How she has become a desolation, a resting place for beasts! Everyone who passes by her will hiss and wave his hand in contempt" (Zep. 2:12-15).

IN THE BOOK OF ZECHARIAH

Sing for Joy and Be Glad, O Daughter of Zion

'"Ho there! Flee from the land of the north,' declares the Lord, 'for I have dispersed you as the four winds of the heavens,' declares the Lord. 'Ho, Zion! Escape, you who are living with the daughter of Babylon.' For thus says the Lord of hosts, 'After glory He has sent me against the nations which plunder you, for he who touches you, touches the apple of His eye. For behold, I will wave My hand over them so that they will be plunder for their slaves. Then you will know that the Lord of hosts has sent Me. Sing for joy and be glad, O daughter of Zion; for behold I am coming and I will dwell in your midst,' declares the Lord. 'Many nations will join themselves to the Lord in that day and will become My people. Then I will dwell in your midst, and you will know that the Lord of hosts has sent Me to you. The Lord will possess Judah as His portion in the holy land, and will again choose Jerusalem'" (Zec. 2:6-12).

Chapter Three

SING IN THE NEW TESTAMENT

IN THE BOOK OF ROMANS

I Will Sing to Your Name

"Therefore, accept one another, just as Christ also accepted us to the glory of God. For I say that Christ has become a servant to the circumcision on behalf of the truth of God to confirm the promises given to the fathers, and for the Gentiles to glorify God for His mercy; as it is written, 'THEREFORE I WILL GIVE PRAISE TO YOU AMONG THE GENTILES, AND I WILL SING TO YOUR NAME.' Again he says, 'REJOICE, O GENTILES, WITH HIS PEOPLE.' And again, 'PRAISE THE LORD ALL YOU GENTILES, AND LET ALL THE PEOPLES PRAISE HIM.' Again Isaiah says, 'THERE SHALL COME THE ROOT OF JESSE, AND HE WHO ARISES TO RULE OVER THE GENTILES, IN HIM SHALL THE GENTILES HOPE.' Now may the God of hope fill you with all joy and peace in believing, so that you will abound in hope by the power of the Holy Spirit" (Ro. 15:7-13).

IN THE BOOK OF 1 CORINTHIANS

I Will Sing with the Spirit

"Therefore let one who speaks in a tongue pray that he may interpret. For if I pray in a tongue, my spirit prays, but my mind is unfruitful. What is the outcome then? I will pray with the spirit and I will pray with the mind also; I will sing with the spirit and I will sing with the mind also. Otherwise if you bless in the spirit only, how will the one who fills the place of the ungifted say the 'Amen' at your giving of thanks, since he does not know what you are saying? For you are giving thanks well enough, but the other person is not edified. I thank God, I speak in tongues more than you all; however, in the church I desire to speak five words with my mind so that I may instruct others also, rather than ten thousand words in a tongue" (1Co. 14:13-19).

IN THE BOOK OF HEBREWS

In the Midst of the Congregation I Will Sing Your Praise

"For it was fitting for Him, for whom are all things, and through whom are all things, in bringing many sons to glory, to perfect the author of their salvation through sufferings. For both He who sanctifies and those who are sanctified are all from one Father; for which reason He is not ashamed to call them brethren, saying, 'I WILL PROCLAIM YOUR NAME TO MY BRETHREN, IN THE MIDST OF THE CONGREGATION I WILL SING YOUR PRAISE.' And again, 'I WILL PUT MY TRUST IN HIM.' And again, 'BEHOLD, I AND THE CHILDREN WHOM GOD HAS

GIVEN ME'" (Heb. 2:10-13).

IN THE BOOK OF JAMES

Is Anyone Cheerful? He Is to Sing Praises

"Is anyone among you suffering? Then he must pray. Is anyone cheerful? He is to sing praises. Is anyone among you sick? Then he must call for the elders of the church and they are to pray over him, anointing him with oil in the name of the Lord; and the prayer offered in faith will restore the one who is sick, and the Lord will raise him up, and if he has committed sins, they will be forgiven him. Therefore, confess your sins to one another, and pray for one another so that you may be healed. The effective prayer of a righteous man can accomplish much. Elijah was a man with a nature like ours, and he prayed earnestly that it would not rain, and it did not rain on the earth for three years and six months. Then he prayed again, and the sky poured rain and the earth produced its fruit" (Jas. 5:13-18).

JOY IN THE OLD TESTAMENT

IN THE BOOK OF GENESIS

I Might Have Sent You Away with Joy

"Laban caught up with Jacob. Now Jacob had pitched his tent in the hill country, and Laban with his kinsmen camped in the hill country of Gilead. Then Laban said to Jacob, 'What have you done by deceiving me and carrying away my daughters like captives of the sword? "Why did you flee secretly and deceive me, and did not tell me so that I might have sent you away with joy and with songs, with timbrel and with lyre; and did not allow me to kiss my sons and my daughters? Now you have done foolishly. It is in my power to do you harm, but the God of your father spoke to me last night, saying, "Be careful not to speak either good or bad to Jacob." Now you have indeed gone away because you longed greatly for your father's house; but why did you steal my gods?' Then Jacob replied to Laban, 'Because I was afraid, for I thought that you would take your daughters from me by force. The one with whom you find your gods shall not live; in the presence of our kinsmen point out what is yours among my belongings and take it for yourself.' For Jacob did not know that Rachel had stolen them" (Gen. 31:25-32).

IN THE BOOK OF DEUTERONOMY

You Did Not Serve the Lord Your God with Joy

"Because you did not serve the Lord your God with joy and a glad heart, for the abundance of all things; therefore you shall serve your enemies whom the Lord will send against you, in hunger, in thirst, in nakedness, and in the lack of all things; and He will put an iron yoke on your neck until He has destroyed you" (De. 28:47-48).

IN THE BOOK OF 1 SAMUEL

To Meet King Saul, with Tambourines and Joy

"It happened as they were coming, when David returned from killing the Philistine, that the women came out of all the cities of Israel, singing and dancing, to meet King Saul, with tambourines, with joy and with musical instruments. The women sang as they played, and said, 'Saul has slain his thousands, And David his ten thousands.' Then Saul became very angry, for this saying displeased him; and he said, 'They have ascribed to David ten thousands, but to me they have ascribed thousands. Now what more can he have but the kingdom?' Saul looked at David with suspicion from that day on" (1Sa. 18:6-9).

Chapter Four

IN THE BOOK OF 1 KINGS

Playing on Flutes and Rejoicing with Great Joy

"Zadok the priest then took the horn of oil from the tent and anointed Solomon. Then they blew the trumpet, and all the people said, 'Long live King Solomon!' All the people went up after him, and the people were playing on flutes and rejoicing with great joy, so that the earth shook at their noise" (1Ki. 1:39-40).

IN THE BOOK OF 1 CHRONICLES

There Was Joy Indeed in Israel

"All these, being men of war who could draw up in battle formation, came to Hebron with a perfect heart to make David king over all Israel; and all the rest also of Israel were of one mind to make David king. They were there with David three days, eating and drinking, for their kinsmen had prepared for them. Moreover those who were near to them, even as far as Issachar and Zebulun and Naphtali, brought food on donkeys, camels, mules and on oxen, great quantities of flour cakes, fig cakes and bunches of raisins, wine, oil, oxen and sheep. There was joy indeed in Israel" (1Ch. 12:38-40).

Chapter Four

Loud-Sounding Cymbals, to Raise Sounds of Joy

"Then David spoke to the chiefs of the Levites to appoint their relatives the singers, with instruments of music, harps, lyres, loud-sounding cymbals, to raise sounds of joy. So the Levites appointed Heman the son of Joel, and from his relatives, Asaph the son of Berechiah; and from the sons of Merari their relatives, Ethan the son of Kushaiah, and with them their relatives of the second rank, Zechariah, Ben, Jaaziel, Shemiramoth, Jehiel, Unni, Eliab, Benaiah, Maaseiah, Mattithiah, Eliphelehu, Mikneiah, Obed-edom and Jeiel, the gatekeepers. So the singers, Heman, Asaph and Ethan were appointed to sound aloud cymbals of bronze; and Zechariah, Aziel, Shemiramoth, Jehiel, Unni, Eliab, Maaseiah and Benaiah, with harps tuned to alamoth; and Mattithiah, Eliphelehu, Mikneiah, Obed-edom, Jeiel and Azaziah, to lead with lyres tuned to the sheminith. Chenaniah, chief of the Levites, was in charge of the singing; he gave instruction in singing because he was skillful. Berechiah and Elkanah were gatekeepers for the ark. Shebaniah, Joshaphat, Nethanel, Amasai, Zechariah, Benaiah and Eliezer, the priests, blew the trumpets before the ark of God. Obed-edom and Jehiah also were gatekeepers for the ark"
(1Ch. 15:16-24).

Chapter Four

Bring Up the Ark of the Covenant with Joy

"So it was David, with the elders of Israel and the captains over thousands, who went to bring up the ark of the covenant of the Lord from the house of Obed-edom with joy. Because God was helping the Levites who were carrying the ark of the covenant of the Lord, they sacrificed seven bulls and seven rams. Now David was clothed with a robe of fine linen with all the Levites who were carrying the ark, and the singers and Chenaniah the leader of the singing with the singers. David also wore an ephod of linen. Thus all Israel brought up the ark of the covenant of the Lord with shouting, and with sound of the horn, with trumpets, with loud-sounding cymbals, with harps and lyres" (1Ch. 15:25-28).

Strength and Joy Are in His Place

"Oh give thanks to the Lord, call upon His name; Make known His deeds among the peoples. Sing to Him, sing praises to Him; Speak of all His wonders. Glory in His holy name; Let the heart of those who seek the Lord be glad. Seek the Lord and His strength; Seek His face continually. Remember His wonderful deeds which He has done, His marvels and the judgments from His mouth, O seed of Israel His servant, Sons of Jacob, His chosen ones! He is the Lord our God; His judgments are in all the earth. Remember His covenant forever, The word which He commanded to a thousand generations, The covenant which He made with Abraham, And His oath to Isaac. He also confirmed it to Jacob for a statute, To Israel as an everlasting covenant, Saying, 'To you I will give the land of Canaan, As the portion of your inheritance.' When they were only a few in number, Very few, and strangers in it, And they wandered about from nation to nation, And from one kingdom to another people, He permitted no man to oppress them, And He reproved kings for their sakes, saying, 'Do not touch My anointed ones, And do My prophets no harm.' Sing to the Lord, all the earth; Proclaim good tidings of His salvation from day to day. Tell of His glory among the nations, His wonderful deeds among all the peoples. For great is the Lord, and greatly to be praised; He also is to be feared above all gods. For all the gods of the peoples are idols, But the Lord made the heavens. Splendor and majesty are before Him, Strength and joy are in His place. Ascribe to the Lord, O families of the peoples, Ascribe to the Lord glory and strength. Ascribe to the Lord the glory due His name; Bring an offering, and come before Him; Worship the Lord in holy array. Tremble before Him, all the earth; Indeed, the world is firmly established, it will not be moved. Let the heavens be glad, and let the earth rejoice; And let them say among the nations, 'The Lord reigns.' Let the sea roar, and all it contains; Let the field exult, and all that is in it. Then the trees of the forest will sing for joy before the Lord; For He is coming to judge the earth. O give thanks to the Lord, for He is good; For His lovingkindness is everlasting. Then say, 'Save us, O God of our salvation, And gather us and deliver us from the nations, To give thanks to Your holy name, And glory in Your praise.' Blessed be the Lord, the God of Israel, From everlasting even to everlasting. Then all the people said, 'Amen,' and praised the Lord" (1Ch. 16:8-36).

With Joy I Have Seen Your People

"But who am I and who are my people that we should be able to offer as generously as this? For all things come from You, and from Your hand we have given You. For we are sojourners before You, and tenants, as all our fathers were; our days on the earth are like a shadow, and there is no hope. O Lord our God, all this abundance that we have provided to build You a house for Your holy name, it is from Your hand, and all is Yours. Since I know, O my God, that You try the heart and delight in uprightness, I, in the integrity of my heart, have willingly offered all these things;so now with joy I have seen Your people, who are present here, make their offerings willingly to You. O Lord, the God of Abraham, Isaac and Israel, our fathers, preserve this forever in the intentions of the heart of Your people, and direct their heart to You; and give to my son Solomon a perfect heart to keep Your commandments, Your testimonies and Your statutes, and to do them all, and to build the temple, for which I have made provision" (1Ch. 29:14-19).

IN THE BOOK OF 2 CHRONICLES

Returning to Jerusalem with Joy

"When Judah came to the lookout of the wilderness, they looked toward the multitude, and behold, they were corpses lying on the ground, and no one had escaped. When Jehoshaphat and his people came to take their spoil, they found much among them, including goods, garments and valuable things which they took for themselves, more than they could carry. And they were three days taking the spoil because there was so much. Then on the fourth day they assembled in the valley of Beracah, for there they blessed the Lord. Therefore they have named that place 'The Valley of Beracah' until today. Every man of Judah and Jerusalem returned with Jehoshaphat at their head, returning to Jerusalem with joy, for the Lord had made them to rejoice over their enemies. They came to Jerusalem with harps, lyres and trumpets to the house of the Lord. And the dread of God was on all the kingdoms of the lands when they heard that the Lord had fought against the enemies of Israel. So the kingdom of Jehoshaphat was at peace, for his God gave him rest on all sides" (2Ch. 20:24-30).

They Sang Praises with Joy, and Bowed Down

"Now at the completion of the burnt offerings, the king and all who were present with him bowed down and worshiped. Moreover, King Hezekiah and the officials ordered the Levites to sing praises to the Lord with the words of David and Asaph the seer. So they sang praises with joy, and bowed down and worshiped" (2Ch. 29:29-30).

Celebrated the Feast of Unleavened Bread with Joy

"Now many people were gathered at Jerusalem to celebrate the Feast of Unleavened Bread in the second month, a very large assembly. They arose and removed the altars which were in Jerusalem; they also removed all the incense altars and cast them into the brook Kidron. Then they slaughtered the Passover lambs on the fourteenth of the second month. And the priests and Levites were ashamed of themselves, and consecrated themselves and brought burnt offerings to the house of the Lord. They stood at their stations after their custom, according to the law of Moses the man of God; the priests sprinkled the blood which they received from the hand of the Levites. For there were many in the assembly who had not consecrated themselves; therefore, the Levites were over the slaughter of the Passover lambs for everyone who was unclean, in order to consecrate them to the Lord. For a multitude of the people, even many from Ephraim and Manasseh, Issachar and Zebulun, had not purified themselves, yet they ate the Passover otherwise than prescribed. For Hezekiah prayed for them, saying, 'May the good Lord pardon everyone who prepares his heart to seek God, the Lord God of his fathers, though not according to the purification rules of the sanctuary.' So the Lord heard Hezekiah and healed the people. The sons of Israel present in Jerusalem celebrated the Feast of Unleavened Bread for seven days with great joy, and the Levites and the priests praised the Lord day after day with loud instruments to the Lord. Then Hezekiah spoke encouragingly to all the Levites who showed good insight in the things of the Lord. So they ate for the appointed seven days, sacrificing peace offerings and giving thanks to the Lord God of their fathers" (2Ch. 30:13-22).

They Celebrated the Seven Days with Joy

"Then the whole assembly decided to celebrate the feast another seven days, so they celebrated the seven days with joy. For Hezekiah king of Judah had contributed to the assembly 1,000 bulls and 7,000 sheep, and the princes had contributed to the assembly 1,000 bulls and 10,000 sheep; and a large number of priests consecrated themselves. All the assembly of Judah rejoiced, with the priests and the Levites and all the assembly that came from Israel, both the sojourners who came from the land of Israel and those living in Judah. So there was great joy in Jerusalem, because there was nothing like this in Jerusalem since the days of Solomon the son of David, king of Israel. Then the Levitical priests arose and blessed the people; and their voice was heard and their prayer came to His holy dwelling place, to heaven" (2Ch. 30:23-27).

IN THE BOOK OF EZRA

Many Shouted Aloud for Joy

"Now when the builders had laid the foundation of the temple of the Lord, the priests stood in their apparel with trumpets, and the Levites, the sons of Asaph, with cymbals, to praise the Lord according to the directions of King David of Israel. They sang, praising and giving thanks to the Lord, saying, 'For He is good, for His lovingkindness is upon Israel forever.' And all the people shouted with a great shout when they praised the Lord because the foundation of the house of the Lord was laid. Yet many of the priests and Levites and heads of fathers' households, the old men who had seen the first temple, wept with a loud voice when the foundation of this house was laid before their eyes, while many shouted aloud for joy, so that the people could not distinguish the sound of the shout of joy from the sound of the weeping of the people, for the people shouted with a loud shout, and the sound was heard far away" (Ezr. 3:10-13).

Celebrated the Dedication of the House of God with Joy

"And the sons of Israel, the priests, the Levites and the rest of the exiles, celebrated the dedication of this house of God with joy. They offered for the dedication of this temple of God 100 bulls, 200 rams, 400 lambs, and as a sin offering for all Israel 12 male goats, corresponding to the number of the tribes of Israel. Then they appointed the priests to their divisions and the Levites in their orders for the service of God in Jerusalem, as it is written in the book of Moses" (Ezr. 6:16-18).

With Joy

"The exiles observed the Passover on the fourteenth of the first month. For the priests and the Levites had purified themselves together; all of them were pure. Then they slaughtered the Passover lamb for all the exiles, both for their brothers the priests and for themselves. The sons of Israel who returned from exile and all those who had separated themselves from the impurity of the nations of the land to join them, to seek the Lord God of Israel, ate the Passover. And they observed the Feast of Unleavened Bread seven days with joy, for the Lord had caused them to rejoice, and had turned the heart of the king of Assyria toward them to encourage them in the work of the house of God, the God of Israel" (Ezr. 6:19-22).

IN THE BOOK OF NEHEMIAH

The Joy of the Lord Is Your Strength

"Then Nehemiah, who was the governor, and Ezra the priest and scribe, and the Levites who taught the people said to all the people, 'This day is holy to the Lord your God; do not mourn or weep.' For all the people were weeping when they heard the words of the law. Then he said to them, 'Go, eat of the fat, drink of the sweet, and send portions to him who has nothing prepared; for this day is holy to our Lord. Do not be grieved, for the joy of the Lord is your strength.' So the Levites calmed all the people, saying, 'Be still, for the day is holy; do not be grieved.' All the people went away to eat, to drink, to send portions and to celebrate a great festival, because they understood the words which had been made known to them" (Ne. 8:9-12).

The Joy of Jerusalem Was Heard from Afar

"Then I had the leaders of Judah come up on top of the wall, and I appointed two great choirs, the first proceeding to the right on top of the wall toward the Refuse Gate. Hoshaiah and half of the leaders of Judah followed them, with Azariah, Ezra, Meshullam,   Judah, Benjamin,

Shemaiah, Jeremiah, and some of the sons of the priests with trumpets; and Zechariah the son of Jonathan, the son of Shemaiah, the son of Mattaniah, the son of Micaiah, the son of Zaccur, the son of Asaph, and his kinsmen, Shemaiah, Azarel, Milalai, Gilalai, Maai, Nethanel, Judah and Hanani, with the musical instruments of David the man of God. And Ezra the scribe went before them. At the Fountain Gate they went directly up the steps of the city of David by the stairway of the wall above the house of David to the Water Gate on the east. The second choir proceeded to the left, while I followed them with half of the people on the wall, above the Tower of Furnaces, to the Broad Wall, and above the Gate of Ephraim, by the Old Gate, by the Fish Gate, the Tower of Hananel and the Tower of the Hundred, as far as the Sheep Gate; and they stopped at the Gate of the Guard. Then the two choirs took their stand in the house of God. So did I and half of the officials with me; and the priests, Eliakim, Maaseiah, Miniamin, Micaiah, Elioenai, Zechariah and Hananiah, with the trumpets; and Maaseiah, Shemaiah, Eleazar, Uzzi, Jehohanan, Malchijah, Elam and Ezer. And the singers sang, with Jezrahiah their leader, and on that day they offered great sacrifices and rejoiced because God had given them great joy, even the women and children rejoiced, so that the joy of Jerusalem was heard from afar" (Ne. 12:31-43).

IN THE BOOK OF ESTHER

There Was Light and Gladness and Joy and Honor

"Then Mordecai went out from the presence of the king in royal robes of blue and white, with a large crown of gold and a garment of fine linen and purple; and the city of Susa shouted and rejoiced. For the Jews there was light and gladness and joy and honor. In each and every province and in each and every city, wherever the king's commandment and his decree arrived, there was gladness and joy for the Jews, a feast and a holiday. And many among the peoples of the land became Jews, for the dread of the Jews had fallen on them" (Es. 8:15-17).

IN THE BOOK OF JOB

Behold, This Is the Joy of His Way

"Can the papyrus grow up without a marsh? Can the rushes grow without water? While it is still green and not cut down, Yet it withers before any other plant. So are the paths of all who forget God; And the hope of the godless will perish, Whose confidence is fragile, And whose trust a spider's web. He trusts in his house, but it does not stand; He holds fast to it, but it does not endure. He thrives before the sun, And his shoots spread out over his garden. His roots wrap around a rock pile, He grasps a house of stones. If he is removed from his place, Then it will deny him, saying, 'I never saw you.' Behold, this is the joy of His way; And out of the dust others will spring. Lo, God will not reject a man of integrity, Nor will He support the evildoers. He will yet fill your mouth with laughter And your lips with shouting. Those who hate you will be clothed with shame, And the tent of the wicked will be no longer" (Job 8:11-22).

And the Joy of the Godless Momentary

"Then Zophar the Naamathite answered, Therefore my disquieting thoughts make me respond, Even because of my inward agitation. I listened to the reproof which insults me, And the spirit of my understanding makes me answer. Do you know this from of old, From the establishment of man on earth, That the triumphing of the wicked is short, And the joy of the godless momentary? Though his loftiness reaches the heavens, And his head touches the clouds, He perishes forever like his refuse; Those who have seen him will say, 'Where is he?' He flies away like a dream, and they cannot find him; Even like a vision of the night he is chased away. The eye which saw him sees him no longer, And his place no longer beholds him. His sons favor the poor, And his hands give back his wealth. His bones are full of his youthful vigor, But it lies down with him in the dust. Though evil is sweet in his mouth

And he hides it under his tongue, Though he desires it and will not let it go, But holds it in his mouth, Yet his food in his stomach is changed To the venom of cobras within him. He swallows riches, But will vomit them up; God will expel them from his belly. He sucks the poison of cobras; The viper's tongue slays him. He does not look at the streams, The rivers flowing with honey and curds. He returns what he has attained And cannot swallow it; As to the riches of his trading, He cannot even enjoy them. For he has oppressed and forsaken the poor; He has seized a house which he has not built" (Job 20:1-19).

I Made the Widow's Heart Sing for Joy

"And Job again took up his discourse and said, 'Oh that I were as in months gone by, As in the days when God watched over me; When His lamp shone over my head, And by His light I walked through darkness; As I was in the prime of my days, When the friendship of God was over my tent; When the Almighty was yet with me, And my children were around me; When my steps were bathed in butter, And the rock poured out for me streams of oil! When I went out to the gate of the city, When I took my seat in the square, The young men saw me and hid themselves, And the old men arose and stood. The princes stopped talking And put their hands on their mouths; The voice of the nobles was hushed, And their tongue stuck to their palate. For when the ear heard, it called me blessed, And when the eye saw, it gave witness of me, Because I delivered the poor who cried for help, And the orphan who had no helper. The blessing of the one ready to perish came upon me, And I made the widow's heart sing for joy. I put on righteousness, and it clothed me; My justice was like a robe and a turban. I was eyes to the blind And feet to the lame. I was a father to the needy, And I investigated the case which I did not know. I broke the jaws of the wicked And snatched the prey from his teeth. Then I thought, "I shall die in my nest, And I shall multiply my days as the sand. My root is spread out to the waters, And dew lies all night on my branch. My glory is ever new with me, And my bow is renewed in my hand'"" (Job 29:1-20).

That He May See His Face with Joy

"If there is an angel as mediator for him, One out of a thousand, To remind a man what is right for him, Then let him be gracious to him, and say, 'Deliver him from going down to the pit, I have found a ransom'; Let his flesh become fresher than in youth, Let him return to the days of his youthful vigor; Then he will pray to God, and He will accept him, That he may see His face with joy, And He may restore His righteousness to man. He will sing to men and say, 'I have sinned and perverted what is right, And it is not proper for me. He has redeemed my soul from going to the pit, And my life shall see the light" (Job 33:23-28).

All the Sons of God Shouted for Joy

"Then the Lord answered Job out of the whirlwind and said, 'Who is this that darkens counsel By words without knowledge? Now gird up your loins like a man, And I will ask you, and you instruct Me! Where were you when I laid the foundation of the earth? Tell Me, if you have understanding, Who set its measurements? Since you know. Or who stretched the line on it? On what were its bases sunk? Or who laid its cornerstone, When the morning stars sang together And all the sons of God shouted for joy'" (Job 38:1-7).

IN THE BOOK OF PSALMS

Let Them Ever Sing for Joy

"But let all who take refuge in You be glad, Let them ever sing for joy; And may You shelter them, That those who love Your name may exult in You. For it is You who blesses the righteous man, O Lord, You surround him with favor as with a shield" (Ps. 5:11-12).

In Your Presence Is Fullness of Joy

"The Lord is the portion of my inheritance and my cup; You support my lot. The lines have fallen to me in pleasant places; Indeed, my heritage is beautiful to me. I will bless the Lord who has counseled me; Indeed, my mind instructs me in the night. I have set the Lord continually before me; Because He is at my right hand, I will not be shaken. Therefore my heart is glad and my glory rejoices; My flesh also will dwell securely. For You will not abandon my soul to Sheol; Nor will You allow Your Holy One to undergo decay. You will make known to me the path of life; In Your presence is fullness of joy; In Your right hand there are pleasures forever" (Ps. 16:5-11).

We Will Sing for Joy Over Your Victory

"May He grant you your heart's desire And fulfill all your counsel! We will sing for joy over your victory, And in the name of our God we will set up our banners. May the Lord fulfill all your petitions" (Ps. 20:4-5).

I Will Offer in His Tent Sacrifices with Shouts of Joy

"One thing I have asked from the Lord, that I shall seek: That I may dwell in the house of the Lord all the days of my life, To behold the beauty of the Lord And to meditate in His temple. For in the day of trouble He will conceal me in His tabernacle; In the secret place of His tent He will hide me; He will lift me up on a rock. And now my head will be lifted up above my enemies around me, And I will offer in His tent sacrifices with shouts of joy; I will sing, yes, I will sing praises to the Lord" (Ps. 27:4-6).

Joy Comes in the Morning

"I will extol You, O Lord, for You have lifted me up, And have not let my enemies rejoice over me. O Lord my God, I cried to You for help, and You healed me. O Lord, You have brought up my soul from Sheol; You have kept me alive, that I would not go down to the pit. Sing praise to the Lord, you His godly ones, And give thanks to His holy name. For His anger is but for a moment, His favor is for a lifetime; Weeping may last for the night, But a shout of joy comes in the morning" (Ps. 30:1-5).

Shout for Joy, All You Who Are Upright in Heart

"I will instruct you and teach you in the way which you should go; I will counsel you with My eye upon you. Do not be as the horse or as the mule which have no understanding, Whose trappings include bit and bridle to hold them in check, Otherwise they will not come near to you. Many are the sorrows of the wicked, But he who trusts in the Lord, lovingkindness shall surround him. Be glad in the Lord and rejoice, you righteous ones; And shout for joy, all you who are upright in heart" (Ps. 32:8-11).

Sing for Joy in the Lord

"Sing for joy in the Lord, O you righteous ones; Praise is becoming to the upright. Give thanks to the Lord with the lyre; Sing praises to Him with a harp of ten strings. Sing to Him a new song; Play skillfully with a shout of joy. For the word of the Lord is upright, And all His work is done in faithfulness. He loves righteousness and justice; The earth is full of the lovingkindness of the Lord" (Ps. 33:1-5).

Let Them Shout for Joy and Rejoice

"Let them shout for joy and rejoice, who favor my vindication; And let them say continually, 'The Lord be magnified, Who delights in the prosperity of His servant.' And my tongue shall declare Your righteousness And Your praise all day long" (Ps. 35:27-28).

With the Voice of Joy and Thanksgiving

"As the deer pants for the water brooks, So my soul pants for You, O God. My soul thirsts for God, for the living God; When shall I come and appear before God? My tears have been my food day and night, While they say to me all day long, 'Where is your God?' These things I remember and I pour out my soul within me. For I used to go along with the throng and lead them in procession to the house of God, With the voice of joy and thanksgiving, a multitude keeping festival" (Ps. 42:1-4).

To God My Exceeding Joy

"O send out Your light and Your truth, let them lead me; Let them bring me to Your holy hill And to Your dwelling places. Then I will go to the altar of God, To God my exceeding joy; And upon the lyre I shall praise You, O God, my God" (Ps. 43:3-4).

God, Has Anointed You with the Oil of Joy

"Your throne, O God, is forever and ever; A scepter of uprightness is the scepter of Your kingdom. You have loved righteousness and hated wickedness; Therefore God, Your God, has anointed You With the oil of joy above Your fellows" (Ps. 45:6-7).

Shout to God with the Voice of Joy

"O clap your hands, all peoples; Shout to God with the voice of joy. For the Lord Most High is to be feared, A great King over all the earth. He subdues peoples under us And nations under our feet. He chooses our inheritance for us, The glory of Jacob whom He loves" (Ps. 47:1-4).

The Joy of the Whole Earth

"Great is the Lord, and greatly to be praised, In the city of our God, His holy mountain. Beautiful in elevation, the joy of the whole earth, Is Mount Zion in the far north, The city of the great King. God, in her palaces, Has made Himself known as a stronghold" (Ps. 48:1-3).

Make Me to Hear Joy and Gladness

"Behold, I was brought forth in iniquity, And in sin my mother conceived me. Behold, You desire truth in the innermost being, And in the hidden part You will make me know wisdom. Purify me with hyssop, and I shall be clean; Wash me, and I shall be whiter than snow. Make me to hear joy and gladness, Let the bones which You have broken rejoice. Hide Your face from my sins And blot out all my iniquities" (Ps. 51:5-9).

Restore to Me the Joy of Your Salvation

"Create in me a clean heart, O God, And renew a steadfast spirit within me. Do not cast me away from Your presence And do not take Your Holy Spirit from me. Restore to me the joy of Your salvation And sustain me with a willing spirit. Then I will teach transgressors Your ways, And sinners will be converted to You" (Ps. 51:10-13).

In the Shadow of Your Wings I Sing for Joy

"When I remember You on my bed, I meditate on You in the night watches, For You have been my help, And in the shadow of Your wings I sing for joy. My soul clings to You; Your right hand upholds me" (Ps. 63:6-8).

You Make the Dawn and the Sunset Shout for Joy

"By awesome deeds You answer us in righteousness, O God of our salvation, You who are the trust of all the ends of the earth and of the farthest sea; Who establishes the mountains by His strength, Being girded with might; Who stills the roaring of the seas, The roaring of their waves, And the tumult of the peoples. They who dwell in the ends of the earth stand in awe of Your signs; You make the dawn and the sunset shout for joy" (Ps. 65:5-8).

They Shout for Joy, Yes, They Sing.

"You visit the earth and cause it to overflow; You greatly enrich it; The stream of God is full of water; You prepare their grain, for thus You prepare the earth. You water its furrows abundantly, You settle its ridges, You soften it with showers, You bless its growth. You have crowned the year with Your bounty, And Your paths drip with fatness. The pastures of the wilderness drip, And the hills gird themselves with rejoicing. The meadows are clothed with flocks And the valleys are covered with grain; They shout for joy, yes, they sing" (Ps. 65:9-13).

Let the Nations be Glad and Sing for Joy

"God be gracious to us and bless us, And cause His face to shine upon us — That Your way may be known on the earth, Your salvation among all nations. Let the peoples praise You, O God; Let all the peoples praise You. Let the nations be glad and sing for joy; For You will judge the peoples with uprightness And guide the nations on the earth. Let the peoples praise You, O God; Let all the peoples praise You. The earth has yielded its produce; God, our God, blesses us. God blesses us, That all the ends of the earth may fear Him" (Ps 67:1-7).

My Lips Will Shout for Joy when I Sing Praises

"I will also praise You with a harp, Even Your truth, O my God; To You I will sing praises with the lyre, O Holy One of Israel. My lips will shout for joy when I sing praises to You; And my soul, which You have redeemed. My tongue also will utter Your righteousness all day long; For they are ashamed, for they are humiliated who seek my hurt" (Ps. 71:22-24).

Chapter Four

Sing for Joy to God Our Strength

"Sing for joy to God our strength; Shout joyfully to the God of Jacob. Raise a song, strike the timbrel, The sweet sounding lyre with the harp. Blow the trumpet at the new moon, At the full moon, on our feast day. For it is a statute for Israel, An ordinance of the God of Jacob. He established it for a testimony in Joseph When he went throughout the land of Egypt. I heard a language that I did not know…" (Ps. 81:1-5).

My Heart and My Flesh Sing for Joy

"How lovely are Your dwelling places, O Lord of hosts! My soul longed and even yearned for the courts of the Lord; My heart and my flesh sing for joy to the living God. The bird also has found a house, And the swallow a nest for herself, where she may lay her young, Even Your altars, O Lord of hosts, My King and my God. How blessed are those who dwell in Your house! They are ever praising You" (Ps. 84:1-4).

All My Springs of Joy Are in You

"His foundation is in the holy mountains. The Lord loves the gates of Zion More than all the other dwelling places of Jacob. Glorious things are spoken of you, O city of God. I shall mention Rahab and Babylon among those who know Me; Behold, Philistia and Tyre with Ethiopia: 'This one was born there.' But of Zion it shall be said, 'This one and that one were born in her'; And the Most High Himself will establish her. The Lord will count when He registers the peoples, 'This one was born there. Then those who sing as well as those who play the flutes shall say, "All my springs of joy are in you"'" (Ps. 87:1-7).

Tabor and Hermon Shout for Joy at Your Name

"The heavens are Yours, the earth also is Yours; The world and all it contains, You have founded them. The north and the south, You have created them; Tabor and Hermon shout for joy at Your name. You have a strong arm; Your hand is mighty, Your right hand is exalted. Righteousness and justice are the foundation of Your throne; Lovingkindness and truth go before You. How blessed are the people who know the joyful sound! O Lord, they walk in the light of Your countenance. In Your name they rejoice all the day, And by Your righteousness they are exalted. For You are the glory of their strength, And by Your favor our horn is exalted. For our shield belongs to the Lord, And our king to the Holy One of Israel" (Ps. 89:11-18).

That We May Sing for Joy and Be Glad

"For we have been consumed by Your anger And by Your wrath we have been dismayed. You have placed our iniquities before

You, Our secret sins in the light of Your presence. For all our days have declined in Your fury; We have finished our years like a sigh. As for the days of our life, they contain seventy years, Or if due to strength, eighty years, Yet their pride is but labor and sorrow; For soon it is gone and we fly away. Who understands the power of Your anger And Your fury, according to the fear that is due You? So teach us to number our days, That we may present to You a heart of wisdom" (Ps. 90:7-12).

I Will Sing for Joy at the Works of Your Hands

"It is good to give thanks to the Lord And to sing praises to Your name, O Most High; To declare Your lovingkindness in the morning And Your faithfulness by night, With the ten-stringed lute and with the harp, With resounding music upon the lyre. For You, O Lord, have made me glad by what You have done, I will sing for joy at the works of Your hands" (Ps. 92:1-4).

O Come, Let Us Sing for Joy

"O come, let us sing for joy to the Lord, Let us shout joyfully to the rock of our salvation. Let us come before His presence with thanksgiving, Let us shout joyfully to Him with psalms. For the Lord is a great God And a great King above all gods, In whose hand are the depths of the earth, The peaks of the mountains are His also. The sea is

His, for it was He who made it, And His hands formed the dry land" (Ps. 95:1-5).

Then All the Trees of the Forest Will Sing for Joy

"Let the heavens be glad, and let the earth rejoice; Let the sea roar, and all it contains; Let the field exult, and all that is in it. Then all the trees of the forest will sing for joy Before the Lord, for He is coming, For He is coming to judge the earth. He will judge the world in righteousness And the peoples in His faithfulness" (Ps. 96:11-13).

Break Forth and Sing for Joy and Sing Praises

"Shout joyfully to the Lord, all the earth; Break forth and sing for joy and sing praises. Sing praises to the Lord with the lyre, With the lyre and the sound of melody. With trumpets and the sound of the horn Shout joyfully before the King, the Lord" (Ps. 98:4-6).

Let the Mountains Sing Together for Joy

"Let the sea roar and all it contains, The world and those who dwell in it. Let the rivers clap their hands, Let the mountains sing together for joy Before the Lord, for He is coming to judge the earth; He will judge the world with righteousness And the peoples with equity" (Ps. 98:7-9).

And He Brought Forth His People with Joy

"Then He brought them out with silver and gold, And among His tribes there was not one who stumbled. Egypt was glad when they departed, For the dread of them had fallen upon them. He spread a cloud for a covering, And fire to illumine by night. They asked, and He brought quail, And satisfied them with the bread of heaven. He opened the rock and water flowed out; It ran in the dry places like a river. For He remembered His holy word With Abraham His servant; And He brought forth His people with joy, His chosen ones with a joyful shout. He gave them also the lands of the nations, That they might take possession of the fruit of the peoples' labor, So that they might keep His statutes And observe His laws, Praise the Lord" (Ps. 105:37-45)!

For They Are the Joy of My Heart

"Your word is a lamp to my feet And a light to my path. I have sworn and I will confirm it, That I will keep Your righteous ordinances. I am exceedingly afflicted; Revive me, O Lord, according to Your word. O accept the freewill offerings of my mouth, O Lord, And teach me Your ordinances. My life is continually in my hand, Yet I do not forget Your law. The wicked have laid a snare for me, Yet I have not gone astray from Your precepts. I have inherited Your testimonies forever, For they are the joy of my heart. I have inclined my heart to perform Your statutes Forever, even to the end" (Ps. 119:105-112).

With a Shout of Joy, Bringing His Sheaves with Him

"Restore our captivity, O Lord, As the streams in the South. Those who sow in tears shall reap with joyful shouting. He who goes to and fro weeping, carrying his bag of seed, Shall indeed come again with a shout of joy, bringing his sheaves with him" (Ps. 126:4-6).

Let Your Godly Ones Sing for Joy

"Behold, we heard of it in Ephrathah, We found it in the field of Jaar. Let us go into His dwelling place; Let us worship at His footstool. Arise, O Lord, to Your resting place, You and the ark of Your strength. Let Your priests be clothed with righteousness, And let Your godly ones sing for joy" (Ps. 132:6-9).

Sing Aloud for Joy

"For the Lord has chosen Zion; He has desired it for His habitation. This is My resting place forever; Here I will dwell, for I have desired it. I will abundantly bless her provision; I will satisfy her needy with bread. Her priests also I will clothe with salvation, And her godly ones will sing aloud for joy. There I will cause the horn of David to spring forth; I have prepared a lamp for Mine anointed. His enemies I will clothe with shame, But upon himself his crown shall shine" (Ps. 132:13-18).

If I Do Not Exalt Jerusalem Above My Chief Joy

"How can we sing the Lord's song In a foreign land? If I forget you, O Jerusalem, May my right hand forget her skill. May my tongue cling to the roof of my mouth If I do not remember you, If I do not exalt Jerusalem Above my chief joy" (Ps. 137:4-6).

Let Them Sing for Joy on Their Beds

"Let the godly ones exult in glory; Let them sing for joy on their beds. Let the high praises of God be in their mouth, And a two-edged sword in their hand, To execute vengeance on the nations And punishment on the peoples, To bind their kings with chains And their nobles with fetters of iron, To execute on them the judgment written; This is an honor for all His godly ones. Praise the Lord" (Ps. 149:5-9).

IN THE BOOK OF PROVERBS

Counselors of Peace Have Joy

"Deceit is in the heart of those who devise evil, But counselors of peace have joy" (Pr. 12:20).

Does Not Share Its Joy

"The heart knows its own bitterness, And a stranger does not share its joy" (Pr. 14:10).

The End of Joy May Be Grief

"Even in laughter the heart may be in pain, And the end of joy may be grief" (Pr. 14:13).

Folly Is Joy to Him Who Lacks Sense

"Folly is joy to him who lacks sense, But a man of understanding walks straight" (Pr. 15:21).

A Man Has Joy in an Apt Answer

"A man has joy in an apt answer, And how delightful is a timely word" (Pr. 15:23)!

The Father of a Fool Has No Joy

"He who sires a fool does so to his sorrow, And the father of a fool has no joy" (Pr. 17:21).

Joy for the Righteous

"The exercise of justice is joy for the righteous, But is terror to the workers of iniquity" (Pr. 21:15).

IN THE BOOK OF ECCLESIASTES

Has Given Wisdom and Knowledge and Joy

"There is nothing better for a man than to eat and drink and tell himself that his labor is good. This also I have seen that it is from the hand of God. For who can eat and who can have enjoyment without Him? For to a person who is good in His sight He has given wisdom and knowledge and joy, while to the sinner He has given the task of gathering and collecting so that he may give to one who is good in God's sight. This too is vanity and striving after wind" (Ec. 2:24-26).

IN THE BOOK OF ISAIAH

Cry Aloud and Shout for Joy

"Then you will say on that day, "I will give thanks to You, O Lord; For although You were angry with me, Your anger is turned away, And You comfort me. Behold, God is my salvation, I will trust and not be afraid; For the Lord God is my strength and song, And He has become my salvation. Therefore you will joyously draw water From the springs of salvation. And in that day you will say, 'Give thanks to the Lord, call on His name. Make known His deeds among the peoples; Make them remember that His name is exalted. Praise the Lord in song, for He has done excellent things; Let this be known throughout the earth. Cry aloud and shout for joy, O inhabitant of Zion, For great in your midst is the Holy One of Israel'" (Isa. 12:1-6).

They Break Forth into Shouts of Joy

"And it will be in the day when the Lord gives you rest from your pain and turmoil and harsh service in which you have been enslaved, that you will take up this taunt against the king of Babylon, and say, 'How the oppressor has ceased, And how fury has ceased! The Lord has broken the staff of the wicked, The scepter of rulers Which used to strike the peoples in fury with unceasing strokes, Which subdued the nations in anger with unrestrained persecution. The whole earth is at rest and is quiet; They break forth into shouts of joy. Even the cypress trees rejoice over you, and the cedars of Lebanon, saying, "Since you were laid low, no tree cutter comes up against us." Sheol from beneath is excited over you to meet you when you come; It arouses for you the spirits of the dead, all the leaders of the earth; It raises all the kings of the nations from their thrones. They will all respond and say to you, "Even you have been made weak as we, You have become like us. Your pomp and the music of your harps Have been brought down to Sheol; Maggots are spread out as your bed beneath you And worms are your covering." How you have fallen from heaven, O star of the morning, son of the dawn! You have been cut down to the earth, You who have weakened the nations! But you said in your heart, "I will ascend to heaven; I will raise my throne above the stars of God, And I will sit on the mount of assembly In the recesses of the north. I will ascend above the heights of the clouds; I will make myself like the Most High." Nevertheless you will be thrust down to Sheol, To the recesses of the pit. Those who see you will gaze at you, They will ponder over you, saying, "Is this the man who made the earth tremble, Who shook kingdoms, Who made the world like a wilderness And overthrew its cities, Who did not allow his prisoners to go home?" All the kings of the nations lie in glory, Each in his own tomb. But you have been cast out of your tomb Like a rejected branch, Clothed with the slain who are pierced with a sword, Who go down to the stones of the pit Like a trampled corpse. You will not be united with them in burial, Because you have ruined your country, You have slain your people. May the offspring of evildoers not be mentioned forever. Prepare for his sons a place of slaughter Because of the iniquity of their fathers. They must not arise and take possession of the earth And fill the face of the world with cities.' 'I will rise up against them,' declares the Lord of hosts, 'and will cut off from Babylon name and survivors, offspring and posterity,' declares the Lord. 'I will also make it a possession for the hedgehog and swamps of water, and I will sweep it with the broom of destruction,' declares the Lord of hosts" (Isa. 14:3-23).

Gladness and Joy

"We have heard of the pride of Moab, an excessive pride; Even of his arrogance, pride, and fury; His idle boasts are false. Therefore Moab will wail; everyone of Moab will wail. You will moan for the raisin cakes of Kir-hareseth As those who are utterly stricken. For the fields of Heshbon have withered, the vines of Sibmah as well;The lords of the nations have trampled down its choice clusters Which reached as far as Jazer and wandered to the deserts; Its tendrils spread themselves out and passed over the sea. Therefore I will weep bitterly for Jazer, for the vine of Sibmah; I will drench you with my tears, O Heshbon and Elealeh; For the shouting over your summer fruits and your harvest has fallen away. Gladness and joy are taken away from the fruitful field; In the vineyards also there will be no cries of joy or jubilant shouting, No treader treads out wine in the presses, For I have made the shouting to cease. Therefore my heart intones like a harp for Moab And my inward feelings for Kir-hareseth. So it will come about when Moab presents himself, When he wearies himself upon his high place And comes to his sanctuary to pray, That he will not prevail" (Isa. 16:6-12).

They Shout for joy

"The new wine mourns, The vine decays, All the merry-hearted sigh. The gaiety of tambourines ceases, The noise of revelers stops, The gaiety of the harp ceases. They do not drink wine with song; Strong drink is bitter to those who drink it. The city of chaos is broken down; Every house is shut up so that none may enter. There is an outcry in the streets concerning the wine; All joy turns to gloom. The gaiety of the earth is banished. Desolation is left in the city And the gate is battered to ruins. For thus it will be in the midst of the earth among the peoples, As the shaking of an olive tree, As the gleanings when the grape harvest is over. They raise their voices, they shout for joy; They cry out from the west concerning the majesty of the Lord. Therefore glorify the Lord in the east, The name of the Lord, the God of Israel, In the coastlands of the sea. From the ends of the earth we hear songs, 'Glory to the Righteous One,' But I say, 'Woe to me! Woe to me! Alas for me! The treacherous deal treacherously, And the treacherous deal very treacherously.' Terror and pit and snare Confront you, O inhabitant of the earth. Then it will be that he who flees the report of disaster will fall into the pit, And he who climbs out of the pit will be caught in the snare; For the windows above are opened, and the foundations of the earth shake. The earth is broken asunder, The earth is split through, The earth is shaken violently. The earth reels to and fro like a drunkard And it totters like a shack, For its transgression is heavy upon it, And it will fall, never to rise again. So it will happen in that day, That the Lord will punish the host of heaven on high, And the kings of the earth on earth. They will be gathered together Like prisoners in the dungeon, And will be confined in prison; And after many days they will be punished. Then the moon will be abashed and the sun ashamed, For the Lord of hosts will reign on Mount Zion and in Jerusalem, And His glory will be before His elders" (Isa. 24:7-23).

Awake and Shout for Joy

"O Lord, Your hand is lifted up yet they do not see it. They see Your zeal for the people and are put to shame; Indeed, fire will devour Your enemies. Lord, You will establish peace for us, Since You have also performed for us all our works. O Lord our God, other masters besides You have ruled us; But through You alone we confess Your name. The dead will not live, the departed spirits will not rise; Therefore You have punished and destroyed them, And You have wiped out all remembrance of them. You have increased the nation, O Lord, You have increased the nation, You are glorified; You have extended all the borders of the land. O Lord, they sought You in distress; They could only whisper a prayer, Your chastening was upon them. As the pregnant woman approaches the time to give birth, She writhes and cries out in her labor pains, Thus were we before You, O Lord. We were pregnant, we writhed in labor, We gave birth, as it seems, only to wind. We could not accomplish deliverance for the earth, Nor were inhabitants of the world born. Your dead will live; Their corpses will rise. You who lie in the dust, awake and shout for joy, For your dew is as the dew of the dawn, And the earth will give birth to the departed spirits" (Isa. 26:11-19).

And Rejoice with Rejoicing and Shout of Joy

"The wilderness and the desert will be glad, And the Arabah will rejoice and blossom; Like the crocus It will blossom profusely And rejoice with rejoicing and shout of joy. The glory of Lebanon will be given to it, The majesty of Carmel and Sharon. They will see the glory of the Lord, The majesty of our God. Encourage the exhausted, and strengthen the feeble. Say to those with anxious heart, 'Take courage, fear not. Behold, your God will come with vengeance; The recompense of God will come, But He will save you.' Then the eyes of the blind will be opened And the ears of the deaf will be unstopped. Then the lame will leap like a deer, And the tongue of the mute will shout for joy. For waters will break forth in the wilderness And streams in the Arabah. The scorched land will become a pool And the thirsty ground springs of water; In the haunt of jackals, its resting place, Grass becomes reeds and rushes. A highway will be there, a roadway, And it will be called the Highway of Holiness. The unclean will not travel on it, But it will be for him who walks that way, And fools will not wander on it. No lion will be there, Nor will any vicious beast go up on it; These will not be found there. But the redeemed will walk there, And the ransomed of the Lord will return And come with joyful shouting to Zion, With everlasting joy upon their heads. They will find gladness and joy, And sorrow and sighing will flee away" (Isa. 35:1-10).

Shout for Joy from the Tops of the Mountains

"Sing to the Lord a new song, Sing His praise from the end of the earth! You who go down to the sea, and all that is in it. You islands, and those who dwell on them. Let the wilderness and its cities lift up their voices, The settlements where Kedar inhabits. Let the inhabitants of Sela sing aloud, Let them shout for joy from the tops of the mountains. Let them give glory to the Lord And declare His praise in the coastlands. The Lord will go forth like a warrior, He will arouse His zeal like a man of war. He will utter a shout, yes, He will raise a war cry. He will prevail against His enemies" (Isa. 42:10-13).

Shout for Joy, O Heavens

"Remember these things, O Jacob, And Israel, for you are My servant; I have formed you, you are My servant, O Israel, you will not be forgotten by Me. I have wiped out your transgressions like a thick cloud And your sins like a heavy mist. Return to Me, for I have redeemed you. Shout for joy, O heavens, for the Lord has done it! Shout joyfully, you lower parts of the earth; Break forth into a shout of joy, you mountains, O forest, and every tree in it; For the Lord has redeemed Jacob And in Israel He shows forth His glory" (Isa. 44:21-23).

Shout for Joy

"Thus says the Lord, 'In a favorable time I have answered You, And in a day of salvation I have helped You; And I will keep You and give You for a covenant of the people, To restore the land, to make them inherit the desolate heritages; Saying to those who are bound, "Go forth," To those who are in darkness, "Show yourselves." Along the roads they will feed, And their pasture will be on all bare heights. They will not hunger or thirst, Nor will the scorching heat or sun strike them down; For He who has compassion on them will lead them And will guide them to springs of water. I will make all My mountains a road, And My highways will be raised up. Behold, these will come from afar; And lo, these will come from the north and from the west, And these from the land of Sinim. Shout for joy, O heavens! And rejoice, O earth! Break forth into joyful shouting, O mountains! For the Lord has comforted His people And will have compassion on His afflicted'" (Isa. 49:8-13).

Joy and Gladness Will Be Found in Her

"Listen to me, you who pursue righteousness, Who seek the Lord: Look to the rock from which you were hewn And to the quarry from which you were dug. Look to Abraham your father And to Sarah who gave birth to you in pain; When he was but one I called him, Then I blessed him and multiplied him. Indeed, the Lord will comfort Zion; He will comfort all her waste places. And her wilderness He will make like Eden, And her desert like the garden of the Lord; Joy and gladness will be found in her, Thanksgiving and sound of a melody" (Isa. 51:1-3).

They Will Obtain Gladness and Joy

"Awake, awake, put on strength, O arm of the Lord; Awake as in the days of old, the generations of long ago. Was it not You who cut Rahab in pieces, Who pierced the dragon? Was it not You who dried up the sea, The waters of the great deep; Who made the depths of the sea a pathway For the redeemed to cross over? So the ransomed of the Lord will return And come with joyful shouting to Zion, And everlasting joy will be on their heads. They will obtain gladness and joy, And sorrow and sighing will flee away" (Isa. 51:9-11).

Shout for Joy, O Barren One

"'Shout for joy, O barren one, you who have borne no child;Break forth into joyful shouting and cry aloud, you who have not travailed; For the sons of the desolate one will be more numerous Than the sons of the married woman,' says the Lord. Enlarge the place of your tent; Stretch out the curtains of your dwellings, spare not; Lengthen your cords And strengthen your pegs. For you will spread abroad to the right and to the left. And your descendants will possess nations And will resettle the desolate cities" (Isa. 54:1-3).

For You Will Go Out with Joy

"Seek the Lord while He may be found; Call upon Him while He is near. Let the wicked forsake his way And the unrighteous man his thoughts; And let him return to the Lord, And He will have compassion on him, And to our God, For He will abundantly pardon. For My thoughts are not your thoughts, Nor are your ways My ways," declares the Lord. For as the heavens are higher than the earth, So are My ways higher than your ways And My thoughts than your thoughts. For as the rain and the snow come down from heaven, And do not return there without watering the earth And making it bear and sprout, And furnishing seed to the sower and bread to the eater; So will My word be which goes forth from My mouth; It will not return to Me empty, Without accomplishing what I desire, And without succeeding in the matter for which I sent it. For you will go out with joy And be led forth with peace; The mountains and the hills will break forth into shouts of joy before you, And all the trees of the field will clap their hands. Instead of the thorn bush the cypress will come up, And instead of the nettle the myrtle will come up, And it will be a memorial to the Lord, For an everlasting sign which will not be cut off" (Isa. 55:6-13).

A Joy from Generation to Generation

"Whereas you have been forsaken and hated With no one passing through, I will make you an everlasting pride, A joy from generation to generation. You will also suck the milk of nations And suck the breast of kings; Then you will know that I, the Lord, am your Savior And your Redeemer, the Mighty One of Jacob. Instead of bronze I will bring gold, And instead of iron I will bring silver, And instead of wood, bronze, And instead of stones, iron. And I will make peace your administrators And righteousness your overseers.

Violence will not be heard again in your land, Nor devastation or destruction within your borders; But you will call your walls salvation, and your gates praise. No longer will you have the sun for light by day, Nor for brightness will the moon give you light; But you will have the Lord for an everlasting light, And your God for your glory. Your sun will no longer set, Nor will your moon wane; For you will have the Lord for an everlasting light, And the days of your mourning will be over. Then all your people will be righteous; They will possess the land forever, The branch of My planting, The work of My hands, That I may be glorified. The smallest one will become a clan, And the least one a mighty nation. I, the Lord, will hasten it in its time" (Isa. 60:15-22).

They Will Shout for Joy Over Their Portion

"Then they will rebuild the ancient ruins, They will raise up the former devastations; And they will repair the ruined cities, The desolations of many generations. Strangers will stand and pasture your flocks, And foreigners will be your farmers and your vinedressers. But you will be called the priests of the Lord; You will be spoken of as ministers of our God. You will eat the wealth of nations, And in their riches you will boast. Instead of your shame you will have a double portion, And instead of humiliation they will shout for joy over their portion. Therefore they will possess a double portion in their land, Everlasting joy will be theirs. For I, the Lord, love justice, I hate robbery in the burnt offering; And I will faithfully give them their recompense And make an everlasting covenant with them. Then their offspring will be known among the nations, And their descendants in the midst of the peoples. All who see them will recognize them Because they are the offspring whom the Lord has blessed" (Isa. 61:4-9).

That We May See Your Joy

"'But he who kills an ox is like one who slays a man; He who sacrifices a lamb is like the one who breaks a dog's neck; He who offers a grain offering is like one who offers swine's blood; He who burns incense is like the one who blesses an idol. As they have chosen their own ways, And their soul delights in their abominations, So I will choose their punishments And will bring on them what they dread. Because I called, but no one answered; I spoke, but they did not listen. And they did evil in My sight And chose that in which I did not delight.' Hear the word of the Lord, you who tremble at His word: 'Your brothers who hate you, who exclude you for My name's sake, Have said, "Let the Lord be glorified, that we may see your joy." But they will be put to shame. A voice of uproar from the city, a voice from the temple, The voice of the Lord who is rendering recompense to His enemies. Before she travailed, she brought forth; Before her pain came, she gave birth to a boy. Who has heard such a thing? Who has seen such things? Can a land be born in one day? Can a nation be brought forth all at once? As soon as Zion travailed, she also brought forth her sons. Shall I bring to the point of birth and not give delivery?' says the Lord. 'Or shall I who gives delivery shut the womb?' says your God. 'Be joyful with Jerusalem and rejoice for her, all you who love her; Be exceedingly glad with her, all you who mourn over her, That you may nurse and be satisfied with her comforting breasts, That you may suck and be delighted with her bountiful bosom.' For thus says the Lord, 'Behold, I extend peace to her like a river, And the glory of the nations like an overflowing stream; And you will be nursed, you will be carried on the hip and fondled on the knees. As one whom his mother comforts, so I will comfort you; And you will be comforted in Jerusalem. Then you will see this, and your heart will be glad, And your bones will flourish like the new grass; And the hand of the Lord will be made known to His servants, But He will be indignant toward His enemies. For behold, the Lord will come in fire And His chariots like the whirlwind, To render His anger with fury, And His rebuke with flames of fire. For the Lord will execute judgment by fire And by His sword on all flesh, And those slain by the Lord will be many. Those who sanctify and purify themselves to go to the gardens, Following one in the center, Who eat swine's flesh, detestable things and mice,

Will come to an end altogether,' declares the Lord" (Isa. 66:3-17).

IN THE BOOK OF JEREMIAH

The Voice of Joy and the Voice of Gladness

"Therefore, behold, days are coming," declares the Lord, "when it will no longer be called Topheth, or the valley of the son of Hinnom, but the valley of the Slaughter; for they will bury in Topheth because there is no other place. The dead bodies of this people will be food for the birds of the sky and for the beasts of the earth; and no one will frighten them away. Then I will make to cease from the cities of Judah and from the streets of Jerusalem the voice of joy and the voice of gladness, the voice of the bridegroom and the voice of the bride; for the land will become a ruin" (Jer. 7:32-34).

Joy and the Delight of My Heart

"You who know, O Lord, Remember me, take notice of me, And take vengeance for me on my persecutors. Do not, in view of Your patience, take me away; Know that for Your sake I endure reproach. Your words were found and I ate them, And Your words became for me a joy and the delight of my heart; For I have been called by Your name, O Lord God of hosts. I did not sit in the circle of merrymakers, Nor did I exult. Because of

Your hand upon me I sat alone, For You filled me with indignation. Why has my pain been perpetual And my wound incurable, refusing to be healed? Will You indeed be to me like a deceptive stream With water that is unreliable" (Jer. 15:15-18)?

The Voice of Joy

"Therefore thus says the Lord of hosts, 'Because you have not obeyed My words, behold, I will send and take all the families of the north,' declares the Lord, 'and I will send to Nebuchadnezzar king of Babylon, My servant, and will bring them against this land and against its inhabitants and against all these nations round about; and I will utterly destroy them and make them a horror and a hissing, and an everlasting desolation. Moreover, I will take from them the voice of joy and the voice of gladness, the voice of the bridegroom and the voice of the bride, the sound of the millstones and the light of the lamp. This whole land will be a desolation and a horror, and these nations will serve the king of Babylon seventy years'" (Jer. 25:8-11).

Shout for Joy on the Height of Zion

"Hear the word of the Lord, O nations, And declare in the coastlands afar off, And say, 'He who scattered Israel will gather him And keep him as a shepherd keeps his flock. For the Lord has ransomed Jacob And redeemed him from the hand of him who was stronger than he. They will come and shout for joy on the height of Zion, And they will be radiant over the bounty of the Lord — Over the grain and the new wine and the oil, And over the young of the flock and the herd; And their life will be like a watered garden, And they will never languish again. Then the virgin will rejoice in the dance, And the young men and the old, together, For I will turn their mourning into joy And will comfort them and give them joy for their sorrow. I will fill the soul of the priests with abundance, And My people will be satisfied with My goodness,' declares the Lord" (Jer. 31:10-14).

A Name of Joy, Praise and Glory

"Then the word of the Lord came to Jeremiah the second time, while he was still confined in the court of the guard, saying, 'Thus says the Lord who made the earth, the Lord who formed it to establish it, the Lord is His name, "Call to Me and I will answer you, and I will tell you great and mighty things, which you do not know." For thus says the Lord God of Israel concerning the houses of this city, and concerning the houses of the kings of Judah which are broken down to make a defense against the siege ramps and against the sword, "While they are coming to fight with the Chaldeans and to fill them with the corpses of men whom I have slain in My anger and in My wrath, and I have hidden My face from this city because of all their wickedness: Behold, I will bring to it health and healing, and I will heal them; and I will reveal to them an abundance of peace and truth. I will restore the fortunes of Judah and the fortunes of Israel and will rebuild them as they were at first. I will cleanse them from all their iniquity by which they have sinned against Me, and I will pardon all their iniquities by which they have sinned against Me and by which they have transgressed against Me. It will be to Me a name of joy, praise and glory before all the nations of the earth which will hear of all the good that I do for them, and they will fear and tremble because of all the good and all the peace that I make for it'"" (Jer. 33:1-9).

The Voice of Joy and the Voice of Gladness

"Thus says the Lord, 'Yet again there will be heard in this place, of which you say, "It is a waste, without man and without beast," that is, in the cities of Judah and in the streets of Jerusalem that are desolate, without man and without inhabitant and without beast, the voice of joy and the voice of gladness, the voice of the bridegroom and the voice of the bride, the voice of those who say, "Give thanks to the Lord of hosts, For the Lord is good, For His lovingkindness is everlasting"; and of those who bring a thank offering into the house of the Lord. For I will restore the fortunes of the land as they were at first,' says the Lord" (Jer. 33:10-11).

Chapter Four

The Town of My Joy!

"Concerning Damascus. 'Hamath and Arpad are put to shame, For they have heard bad news; They are disheartened. There is anxiety by the sea, It cannot be calmed. Damascus has become helpless; She has turned away to flee, And panic has gripped her; Distress and pangs have taken hold of her Like a woman in childbirth. How the city of praise has not been deserted, The town of My joy! Therefore, her young men will fall in her streets, And all the men of war will be silenced in that day,' declares the Lord of hosts. 'I will set fire to the wall of Damascus, And it will devour the fortified towers of Ben-hadad" (Jer. 49:23-27).

Will Shout for Joy over Babylon

"'Come forth from her midst, My people, And each of you save yourselves From the fierce anger of the Lord. Now so that your heart does not grow faint, And you are not afraid at the report that will be heard in the land — For the report will come one year, And after that another report in another year, And violence will be in the land With ruler against ruler — Therefore behold, days are coming When I will punish the idols of Babylon; And her whole land will be put to shame And all her slain will fall in her midst. Then heaven and earth and all that is in them Will shout for joy over Babylon, For the destroyers will come to her from the north,' Declares the Lord" (Jer. 51:45-48).

IN THE BOOK OF EZEKIEL

The Joy of Their Pride

"As for you, son of man, will it not be on the day when I take from them their stronghold, the joy of their pride, the desire of their eyes and their heart's delight, their sons and their daughters, that on that day he who escapes will come to you with information for your ears? On that day your mouth will be opened to him who escaped, and you will speak and be mute no longer. Thus you will be a sign to them, and they will know that I am the Lord" (Eze. 24:25-27).

IN THE BOOK OF JOEL

Gladness and Joy from the House of Our God

"Gird yourselves with sackcloth And lament, O priests; Wail, O ministers of the altar! Come, spend the night in sackcloth O ministers of my God, For the grain offering and the drink offering Are withheld from the house of your God. Consecrate a fast, Proclaim a solemn assembly; Gather the elders And all the inhabitants of the land To the house of the Lord your God, And cry out to the Lord. Alas for the day! For the day of the Lord is near, And it will come as destruction from the Almighty. Has not food been cut off before our eyes, Gladness and joy from the house of our God? The seeds shrivel under their clods; The storehouses are desolate, The barns are torn down, For the grain is dried up. How the beasts groan! The herds of cattle wander aimlessly Because there is no pasture for them; Even the flocks of sheep suffer. To You, O Lord, I cry; For fire has devoured the pastures of the wilderness And the flame has burned up all the trees of the field. Even the beasts of the field pant for You; For the water brooks are dried up And fire has devoured the pastures of the wilderness" (Joel 1:13-20).

IN THE BOOK OF ZEPHANIAH

Shout for Joy, O Daughter of Zion

"Shout for joy, O daughter of Zion! Shout in triumph, O Israel! Rejoice and exult with all your heart, O daughter of Jerusalem! The Lord has taken away His judgments against you, He has cleared away your enemies. The King of Israel, the Lord, is in your midst; You will fear disaster no more. In that day it will be said to Jerusalem: 'Do not be afraid, O Zion; Do not let your hands fall limp. The Lord your God is in your midst, A victorious warrior. He will exult over you with joy, He will be quiet in His love, He will rejoice over you with shouts of joy. I will gather those who grieve about the appointed feasts — They came from you, O Zion; The reproach of exile is a burden on them. Behold, I am going to deal at that time With all your oppressors, I will save the lame And gather the outcast, And I will turn their shame into praise and renown In all the earth. At that time I will bring you in, Even at the time when I gather you together; Indeed, I will give you renown and praise Among all the peoples of the earth, When I restore your fortunes before your eyes,' Says the Lord" (Zep. 3:14-20).

IN THE BOOK OF ZECHARIAH

Sing for Joy and be Glad

"'Ho there! Flee from the land of the north,' declares the Lord, 'for I have dispersed you as the four winds of the heavens,' declares the Lord. Ho, Zion! Escape, you who are living with the daughter of Babylon. For thus says the Lord of hosts, 'After glory He has sent me against the nations which plunder you, for he who touches you, touches the apple of His eye. For behold, I will wave My hand over them so that they will be plunder for their slaves. Then you will know that the Lord of hosts has sent Me. Sing for joy and be glad, O daughter of Zion; for behold I am coming and I will dwell in your midst,' declares the Lord. Many nations will join themselves to the Lord in that day and will become My people. Then I will dwell in your midst, and you will know that the Lord of hosts has sent Me to you. The Lord will possess Judah as His portion in the holy land, and will again choose Jerusalem" (Zec. 2:6-12).

Will Become Joy, Gladness, and Cheerful Feasts

"Then the word of the Lord of hosts came to me, saying, Thus says the Lord of hosts, 'The fast of the fourth, the fast of the fifth, the fast of the seventh and the fast of the tenth months will become joy, gladness, and cheerful feasts for the house of Judah; so love truth and peace'" (Zec. 8:18-19).

JOY IN THE NEW TESTAMENT

IN THE BOOK OF MATTHEW

They Rejoiced Exceedingly with Great Joy

"Then Herod secretly called the magi and determined from them the exact time the star appeared. And he sent them to Bethlehem and said, 'Go and search carefully for the Child; and when you have found Him, report to me, so that I too may come and worship Him.' After hearing the king, they went their way; and the star, which they had seen in the east, went on before them until it came and stood over the place where the Child was. When they saw the star, they rejoiced exceedingly with great joy. After coming into the house they saw the Child with Mary His mother; and they fell to the ground and worshiped Him. Then, opening their treasures, they presented to Him gifts of gold, frankincense, and myrrh. And having been warned by God in a dream not to return to Herod, the magi left for their own country by another way" (Mt. 2:7-12).

Immediately Receives It with Joy

"Hear then the parable of the sower. When anyone hears the word of the kingdom and does not understand it, the evil one comes and snatches away what has been sown in his heart. This is the one on whom seed was sown beside the road. The one on whom seed was sown on the rocky places, this is the man who hears the word and immediately receives it with joy; yet he has no firm root in himself, but is only temporary, and when affliction or persecution arises because of the word, immediately he falls away. And the one on whom seed was sown among the thorns, this is the man who hears the word, and the worry of the world and the deceitfulness of wealth choke the word, and it becomes unfruitful. And the one on whom seed was sown on the good soil, this is the man who hears the word and understands it; who indeed bears fruit and brings forth, some a hundredfold, some sixty, and some thirty" (Mt. 13:18-23).

From Joy over It

"The kingdom of heaven is like a treasure hidden in the field, which a man found and hid again; and from joy over it he goes and sells all that he has and buys that field" (Mt. 13:44).

Enter into the Joy of Your Master

"Now after a long time the master of those slaves *came and *settled accounts with them. The one who had received the five talents came up and brought five more talents, saying, 'Master, you entrusted five talents to me. See, I have gained five more talents.' His master said to him, 'Well done, good and faithful slave. You were faithful with a few things, I will put you in charge of many things; enter into the joy of your master" (Mt. 25:19-21).

Enter into the Joy of Your Master

"Also the one who had received the two talents came up and said, 'Master, you entrusted two talents to me. See, I have gained two more talents.' His master said to him, 'Well done, good and faithful slave. You were faithful with a few things, I will put you in charge of many things; enter into the joy of your master" (Mt. 25:22-23).

With Fear and Great Joy

"And they left the tomb quickly with fear and great joy and ran to report it to His disciples. And behold, Jesus met them and greeted them. And they came up and took hold of His feet and worshiped Him. Then Jesus *said to them, 'Do not be afraid; go and take word to My brethren to leave for Galilee, and there they will see Me'" (Mt. 28:8-10).

IN THE BOOK OF MARK

Immediately Receive It with Joy

"And He said to them, 'Do you not understand this parable? How will you understand all the parables? The sower sows the word. These are the ones who are beside the road where the word is sown; and when they hear, immediately Satan comes and takes away the word which has been sown in them. In a similar way these are the ones on whom seed was sown on the rocky places, who, when they hear the word, immediately receive it with joy; and they have no firm root in themselves, but are only temporary; then, when affliction or persecution arises because of the word, immediately they fall away. And others are the ones on whom seed was sown among the thorns; these are the ones who have heard the word, but the worries of the world, and the deceitfulness of riches, and the desires for other things enter in and choke the word, and it becomes unfruitful. And those are the ones on whom seed was sown on the good soil; and they hear the word and accept it and bear fruit, thirty, sixty, and a hundredfold'" (Mr. 4:13-20).

IN THE BOOK OF LUKE

You Will Have Joy and Gladness

"Now it happened that while he was performing his priestly service before God in the appointed order of his division, according to the custom of the priestly office, he was chosen by lot to enter the temple of the Lord and burn incense. And the whole multitude of the people were in prayer outside at the hour of the incense offering. And an angel of the Lord appeared to him, standing to the right of the altar of incense. Zacharias was troubled when he saw the angel, and fear gripped him. But the angel said to him, 'Do not be afraid, Zacharias, for your petition has been heard, and your wife Elizabeth will bear you a son, and you will give him the name John. You will have joy and gladness, and many will rejoice at his birth. For he will be great in the sight of the Lord; and he will drink no wine or liquor, and he will be filled with the Holy Spirit while yet in his mother's womb. And he will turn many of the sons of Israel back to the Lord their God. It is he who will go as a forerunner before Him in the spirit and power of Elijah, TO TURN THE HEARTS OF THE FATHERS BACK TO THE CHILDREN, and the disobedient to the attitude of the righteous, so as to make ready a people prepared for the Lord'" (Lk. 1:8-17).

The Baby Leaped in My Womb for Joy

"Now at this time Mary arose and went in a hurry to the hill country, to a city of Judah, and entered the house of Zacharias and greeted Elizabeth. When Elizabeth heard Mary's greeting, the baby leaped in her womb; and Elizabeth was filled with the Holy Spirit. And she cried out with a loud voice and said, 'Blessed are you among women, and blessed is the fruit of your womb! And how has it happened to me, that the mother of my Lord would come to me? For behold, when the sound of your greeting reached my ears, the baby leaped in my womb for joy. And blessed is she who believed that there would be a fulfillment of what had been spoken to her by the Lord'" (Lk. 1:39-45).

I Bring You Good News of Great Joy

"In the same region there were some shepherds staying out in the fields and keeping watch over their flock by night. And an angel of the Lord suddenly stood before them, and the glory of the Lord shone around them; and they were terribly frightened. But the angel said to them, 'Do not be afraid; for behold, I bring you good news of great joy which will be for all the people; for today in the city of David there has been born for you a Savior, who is Christ the Lord. This will be a sign for you: you will find a baby wrapped in cloths and lying in a manger. And suddenly there appeared with the angel a multitude of the heavenly host praising God and saying, Glory to God in the highest, And on earth peace among men with whom He is pleased'" (Lk. 2:8-14).

Be Glad in that Day and Leap for Joy

"And turning His gaze toward His disciples, He began to say, "Blessed are you who are poor, for yours is the kingdom of God. 'Blessed are you who hunger now, for you shall be satisfied. Blessed are you who weep now, for you shall laugh. Blessed are you when men hate you, and ostracize you, and insult you, and scorn your name as evil, for the sake of the Son of Man. Be glad in that day and leap for joy, for behold, your reward is great in heaven. For in the same way their fathers used to treat the prophets. But woe to you who are rich, for you are receiving your comfort in full. Woe to you who are well-fed now, for you shall be hungry. Woe to you who laugh now, for you shall mourn and weep. Woe to you when all men speak well of you, for their fathers used to treat the false prophets in the same way'" (Lk. 6:20-26).

Receive the Word with Joy

"Now the parable is this: the seed is the word of God. Those beside the road are those who have heard; then the devil comes and takes away the word from their heart, so that they will not believe and be saved. Those on the rocky soil are those who, when they hear, receive the word with joy; and these have no firm root; they believe for a while, and in time of temptation fall away. The seed which fell among the thorns, these are the ones who have heard, and as they go on their way they are choked with worries and riches and pleasures of this life, and bring no fruit to maturity. But the seed in the good soil, these are the ones who have heard the word in an honest and good heart, and hold it fast, and bear fruit with perseverance" (Lk. 8:11-15).

Chapter Five

The Seventy Returned with Joy

"The seventy returned with joy, saying, 'Lord, even the demons are subject to us in Your name.' And He said to them, 'I was watching Satan fall from heaven like lightning. Behold, I have given you authority to tread on serpents and scorpions, and over all the power of the enemy, and nothing will injure you. Nevertheless do not rejoice in this, that the spirits are subject to you, but rejoice that your names are recorded in heaven'" (Lk. 10:17-20).

More Joy in Heaven over One Sinner Who Repents

"So He told them this parable, saying, 'What man among you, if he has a hundred sheep and has lost one of them, does not leave the ninety-nine in the open pasture and go after the one which is lost until he finds it? When he has found it, he lays it on his shoulders, rejoicing. And when he comes home, he calls together his friends and his neighbors, saying to them, "Rejoice with me, for I have found my sheep which was lost!" I tell you that in the same way, there will be more joy in heaven over one sinner who repents than over ninety-nine righteous persons who need no repentance'" (Lk. 15:3-7).

There Is Joy in the Presence of the Angels of God

"Or what woman, if she has ten silver coins and loses one coin, does not light a lamp and sweep the house and search carefully until she finds it? When she has found it, she calls together her friends and neighbors, saying, 'Rejoice with me, for I have found the coin which I had lost!' In the same way, I tell you, there is joy in the presence of the angels of God over one sinner who repents" (Lk. 15:8-10).

Their Joy and Amazement

"While they were telling these things, He Himself stood in their midst and said to them, 'Peace be to you.' But they were startled and frightened and thought that they were seeing a spirit. And He said to them, 'Why are you troubled, and why do doubts arise in your hearts? See My hands and My feet, that it is I Myself; touch Me and see, for a spirit does not have flesh and bones as you see that I have.' And when He had said this, He showed them His hands and His feet. While they still could not believe it because of their joy and amazement, He said to them, 'Have you anything here to eat?" They gave Him a piece of a broiled fish; and He took it and ate it before them" (Lk. 24:36-43).

Returned to Jerusalem with Great Joy

"And He led them out as far as Bethany, and He lifted up His hands and blessed them. While He was blessing them, He parted from them and was carried up into heaven. And they, after worshiping Him, returned to Jerusalem with great joy, and were continually in the temple praising God" (Lk. 24:50-53).

IN THE BOOK OF JOHN

Your Joy May Be Made Full

"I am the true vine, and My Father is the vinedresser. Every branch in Me that does not bear fruit, He takes away; and every branch that bears fruit, He prunes it so that it may bear more fruit. You are already clean because of the word which I have spoken to you. Abide in Me, and I in you. As the branch cannot bear fruit of itself unless it abides in the vine, so neither can you unless you abide in Me. I am the vine, you are the branches; he who abides in Me and I in him, he bears much fruit, for apart from Me you can do nothing. If anyone does not abide in Me, he is thrown away as a branch and dries up; and they gather them, and cast them into the fire and they are burned. If you abide in Me, and My words abide in you, ask whatever you wish, and it will be done for you. My Father is glorified by this, that you bear much fruit, and so prove to be My disciples. Just as the Father has loved Me, I have also loved you; abide in My love. If you keep My commandments, you will abide in My love; just as I have kept My Father's commandments and abide in His love. These things I have spoken to you so that My joy may be in you, and that your joy may be made full" (Jn. 15:1-11).

Your Grief Will Be Turned into Joy

"'A little while, and you will no longer see Me; and again a little while, and you will see Me.' Some of His disciples then said to one another, 'What is this thing He is telling us, "A little while, and you will not see Me; and again a little while, and you will see Me"; and, "because I go to the Father"? 'So they were saying, 'What is this that He says, "A little while"? We do not know what He is talking about.' Jesus knew that they wished to question Him, and He said to them, 'Are you deliberating together about this, that I said, "A little while, and you will not see Me, and again a little while, and you will see Me"? Truly, truly, I say to you, that you will weep and lament, but the world will rejoice; you will grieve, but your grief will be turned into joy. Whenever a woman is in labor she has pain, because her hour has come; but when she gives birth to the child, she no longer remembers the anguish because of the joy that a child has been born into the world. Therefore you too have grief now; but I will see you again, and your heart will rejoice, and no one will take your joy away from you. In that day you will not question Me about anything. Truly, truly, I say to you, if you ask the Father for anything in My name, He will give it to you. Until now you have asked for nothing in My name; ask and you will receive, so that your joy may be made full'" (Jn. 16:16-24).

My Joy

"I have manifested Your name to the men whom You gave Me out of the world; they were Yours and You gave them to Me, and they have kept Your word. Now they have come to know that everything You have given Me is from You; for the words which You gave Me I have given to them; and they received them and truly understood that I came forth from You, and they believed that You sent Me. I ask on their behalf; I do not ask on behalf of the world, but of those whom You have given Me; for they are Yours; and all things that are Mine are Yours, and Yours are Mine; and I have been glorified in them. I am no longer in the world; and yet they themselves are in the world, and I come to You. Holy Father, keep them in Your name, the name which You have given Me, that they may be one even as We are. While I was with them, I was keeping them in Your name which You have given Me; and I guarded them and not one of them perished but the son of perdition, so that the Scripture would be fulfilled. But now I come to You; and these things I speak in the world so that they may have My joy made full in themselves. I have given them Your word; and the world has hated them, because they are not of the world, even as I am not of the world. I do not ask You to take them out of the world, but to keep them from the evil one. They are not of the world, even as I am not of the world. Sanctify them in the truth; Your word is truth. As You sent Me into the world, I also have sent them into the world. For their sakes I sanctify Myself, that they themselves also may be sanctified in truth" (Jn. 17:6-19).

IN THE BOOK OF ACTS

Because of Her Joy

"On the very night when Herod was about to bring him forward, Peter was sleeping between two soldiers, bound with two chains, and guards in front of the door were watching over the prison. And behold, an angel of the Lord suddenly appeared and a light shone in the cell; and he struck Peter's side and woke him up, saying, 'Get up quickly.' And his chains fell off his hands. And the angel said to him, 'Gird yourself and put on your sandals.' And he did so. And he said to him, 'Wrap your cloak around you and follow me.' And he went out and continued to follow, and he did not know that what was being done by the angel was real, but thought he was seeing a vision. When they had passed the first and second guard, they came to the iron gate that leads into the city, which opened for them by itself; and they went out and went along one street, and immediately the angel departed from him. When Peter came to himself, he said, 'Now I know for sure that the Lord has sent forth His angel and rescued me from the hand of Herod and from all that the Jewish people were expecting.' And when he realized this, he went to the house of Mary, the mother of John who was also called Mark, where many were gathered together and were praying. When he knocked at the door of the gate, a servant-girl named Rhoda came to answer. When she recognized Peter's voice, because of her joy she did not open the gate, but ran in and announced that Peter was standing in front of the gate. They said to her, 'You are out of your mind!' But she kept insisting that it was so. They kept saying, 'It is his angel.' But Peter continued knocking; and when they had opened the door, they saw him and were amazed. But motioning to them with his hand to be silent, he described to them how the Lord had led him out of the prison. And he said, 'Report these things to James and the brethren.' Then he left and went to another place" (Ac. 12:6-17).

Filled with Joy and with the Holy Spirit

"When the Gentiles heard this, they began rejoicing and glorifying the word of the Lord; and as many as had been appointed to eternal life believed. And the word of the Lord was being spread through the whole region. But the Jews incited the devout women of prominence and the leading men of the city, and instigated a persecution against Paul and Barnabas, and drove them out of their district. But they shook off the dust of their feet in protest against them and went to Iconium. And the disciples were continually filled with joy and with the Holy Spirit" (Ac. 13:48-52).

Bringing Great Joy to All the Brethren

"Some men came down from Judea and began teaching the brethren, Unless you are circumcised according to the custom of Moses, you cannot be saved. And when Paul and Barnabas had great dissension and debate with them, the brethren determined that Paul and Barnabas and some others of them should go up to Jerusalem to the apostles and elders concerning this issue. Therefore, being sent on their way by the church, they were passing through both Phoenicia and Samaria, describing in detail the conversion of the Gentiles, and were bringing great joy to all the brethren. When they arrived at Jerusalem, they were received by the church and the apostles and the elders, and they reported all that God had done with them. But some of the sect of the Pharisees who had believed stood up, saying, 'It is necessary to circumcise them and to direct them to observe the Law of Moses'" (Ac. 15:1-5).

IN THE BOOK OF ROMANS

Righteousness and Peace and Joy in the Holy Spirit

"Therefore let us not judge one another anymore, but rather determine this — not to put an obstacle or a stumbling block in a brother's way. I know and am convinced in the Lord Jesus that nothing is unclean in itself; but to him who thinks anything to be unclean, to him it is unclean. For if because of food your brother is hurt, you are no longer walking according to love. Do not destroy with your food him for whom Christ died. Therefore do not let what is for you a good thing be spoken of as evil; for the kingdom of God is not eating and drinking, but righteousness and peace and joy in the Holy Spirit. For he who in this way serves Christ is acceptable to God and approved by men. So then we pursue the things which make for peace and the building up of one another. Do not tear down the work of God for the sake of food. All things indeed are clean, but they are evil for the man who eats and gives offense. It is good not to eat meat or to drink wine, or to do anything by which your brother stumbles. The faith which you have, have as your own conviction before God. Happy is he who does not condemn himself in what he approves. But he who doubts is condemned if he eats, because his eating is not from faith; and whatever is not from faith is sin" (Ro. 14:13-23).

Fill You with All Joy and Peace in Believing

"Therefore, accept one another, just as Christ also accepted us to the glory of God. For I say that Christ has become a servant to the circumcision on behalf of the truth of God to confirm the promises given to the fathers, and for the Gentiles to glorify God for His mercy; as it is written, 'THEREFORE I WILL GIVE PRAISE TO YOU AMONG THE GENTILES, AND I WILL SING TO YOUR NAME.' Again he says, 'REJOICE, O GENTILES, WITH HIS PEOPLE.' And again, 'PRAISE THE LORD ALL YOU GENTILES, AND LET ALL THE PEOPLES PRAISE HIM.' Again Isaiah says, 'THERE SHALL COME THE ROOT OF JESSE, AND HE WHO ARISES TO RULE OVER THE GENTILES, IN HIM SHALL THE GENTILES HOPE.' Now may the God of hope fill you with all joy and peace in believing, so that you will abound in hope by the power of the Holy Spirit" (Ro. 15:7-13).

Come to You in Joy

"Now I urge you, brethren, by our Lord Jesus Christ and by the love of the Spirit, to strive together with me in your prayers to God for me, that I may be rescued from those who are disobedient in Judea, and that my service for Jerusalem may prove acceptable to the saints; so that I may come to you in joy by the will of God and find refreshing rest in your company. Now the God of peace be with you all. Amen" (Ro. 15:30-33).

IN THE BOOK OF 2 CORINTHIANS

Are Workers with You for Your Joy

"But I call God as witness to my soul, that to spare you I did not come again to Corinth. Not that we lord it over your faith, but are workers with you for your joy; for in your faith you are standing firm" (2Co. 1:23-24).

My Joy Would Be the Joy of You All

"But I determined this for my own sake, that I would not come to you in sorrow again. For if I cause you sorrow, who then makes me glad but the one whom I made sorrowful? This is the very thing I wrote you, so that when I came, I would not have sorrow from those who ought to make me rejoice; having confidence in you all that my joy would be the joy of you all. For out of much affliction and anguish of heart I wrote to you with many tears; not so that you would be made sorrowful, but that you might know the love which I have especially for you" (2Co. 2:1-4).

I Am Overflowing with Joy in All Our Affliction

"Make room for us in your hearts; we wronged no one, we corrupted no one, we took advantage of no one. I do not speak to condemn you, for I have said before that you are in our hearts to die together and to live together. Great is my confidence in you; great is my boasting on your behalf. I am filled with comfort; I am overflowing with joy in all our affliction" (2Co. 7:2-4).

Abundance of Joy

"Now, brethren, we wish to make known to you the grace of God which has been given in the churches of Macedonia, that in a great ordeal of affliction their abundance of joy and their deep poverty overflowed in the wealth of their liberality. For I testify that according to their ability, and beyond their ability, they gave of their own accord, begging us with much urging for the favor of participation in the support of the saints, and this, not as we had expected, but they first gave themselves to the Lord and to us by the will of God. So we urged Titus that as he had previously made a beginning, so he would also complete in you this gracious work as well" (2Co. 8:1-6).

Chapter Five

IN THE BOOK OF GALATIANS

The Fruit of the Spirit Is Love

"But I say, walk by the Spirit, and you will not carry out the desire of the flesh. For the flesh sets its desire against the Spirit, and the Spirit against the flesh; for these are in opposition to one another, so that you may not do the things that you please. But if you are led by the Spirit, you are not under the Law. Now the deeds of the flesh are evident, which are: immorality, impurity, sensuality, idolatry, sorcery, enmities, strife, jealousy, outbursts of anger, disputes, dissensions, factions, envying, drunkenness, carousing, and things like these, of which I forewarn you, just as I have forewarned you, that those who practice such things will not inherit the kingdom of God. But the fruit of the Spirit is love, joy, peace, patience, kindness, goodness, faithfulness, gentleness, self-control; against such things there is no law. Now those who belong to Christ Jesus have crucified the flesh with its passions and desires" (Gal. 5:16-24).

IN THE BOOK OF PHILIPPIANS

Offering Prayer with Joy

"I thank my God in all my remembrance of you, always offering prayer with joy in my every prayer for you all, in view of your participation in the gospel from the first day until now. For I am confident of this very thing, that He who began a good work in you will perfect it until the day of Christ Jesus. For it is only right for me to feel this way about you all, because I have you in my heart, since both in my imprisonment and in the defense and confirmation of the gospel, you all are partakers of grace with me. For God is my witness, how I long for you all with the affection of Christ Jesus. And this I pray, that your love may abound still more and more in real knowledge and all discernment, so that you may approve the things that are excellent, in order to be sincere and blameless until the day of Christ; having been filled with the fruit of righteousness which comes through Jesus Christ, to the glory and praise of God" (Php. 1:3-11).

Make My Joy Complete

"Therefore if there is any encouragement in Christ, if there is any consolation of love, if there is any fellowship of the Spirit, if any affection and compassion, make my joy complete by being of the same mind, maintaining the same love, united in spirit, intent on one purpose. Do nothing from selfishness or empty conceit, but with humility of mind regard one another as more important than yourselves; do not merely look out for your own personal interests, but also for the interests of others. Have this attitude in yourselves which was also in Christ Jesus, who, although He existed in the form of God, did not regard equality with God a thing to be grasped, but emptied Himself, taking the form of a bond-servant, and being made in the likeness of men. Being found in appearance as a man, He humbled Himself by becoming obedient to the point of death, even death on a cross. For this reason also, God highly exalted Him, and bestowed on Him the name which is above every name, so that at the name of Jesus EVERY KNEE WILL BOW, of those who are in heaven and on earth and under the earth, and that every tongue will confess that Jesus Christ is Lord, to the glory of God the Father" (Php. 2:1-11).

I Rejoice and Share My Joy with You All

"Do all things without grumbling or disputing; so that you will prove yourselves to be blameless and innocent, children of God above reproach in the midst of a crooked and perverse generation, among whom you appear as lights in the world, holding fast the word of life, so that in the day of Christ I will have reason to glory because I did not run in vain nor toil in vain. But even if I am being poured out as a drink offering upon the sacrifice and service of your faith, I rejoice and share my joy with you all. You too, I urge you, rejoice in the same way and share your joy with me" (Php. 2:14-18).

Chapter Five

With All Joy

"But I hope in the Lord Jesus to send Timothy to you shortly, so that I also may be encouraged when I learn of your condition. For I have no one else of kindred spirit who will genuinely be concerned for your welfare. For they all seek after their own interests, not those of Christ Jesus. But you know of his proven worth, that he served with me in the furtherance of the gospel like a child serving his father. Therefore I hope to send him immediately, as soon as I see how things go with me; and I trust in the Lord that I myself also will be coming shortly. But I thought it necessary to send to you Epaphroditus, my brother and fellow worker and fellow soldier, who is also your messenger and minister to my need; because he was longing for you all and was distressed because you had heard that he was sick. For indeed he was sick to the point of death, but God had mercy on him, and not on him only but also on me, so that I would not have sorrow upon sorrow. Therefore I have sent him all the more eagerly so that when you see him again you may rejoice and I may be less concerned about you. Receive him then in the Lord with all joy, and hold men like him in high regard; because he came close to death for the work of Christ, risking his life to complete what was deficient in your service to me" (Php. 2:19-30).

Chapter Five

IN THE BOOK OF 1 THESSALONIANS

With the Joy of the Holy Spirit

"We give thanks to God always for all of you, making mention of you in our prayers; constantly bearing in mind your work of faith and labor of love and steadfastness of hope in our Lord Jesus Christ in the presence of our God and Father, knowing, brethren beloved by God, His choice of you; for our gospel did not come to you in word only, but also in power and in the Holy Spirit and with full conviction; just as you know what kind of men we proved to be among you for your sake. You also became imitators of us and of the Lord, having received the word in much tribulation with the joy of the Holy Spirit, so that you became an example to all the believers in Macedonia and in Achaia. For the word of the Lord has sounded forth from you, not only in Macedonia and Achaia, but also in every place your faith toward God has gone forth, so that we have no need to say anything. For they themselves report about us what kind of a reception we had with you, and how you turned to God from idols to serve a living and true God, and to wait for His Son from heaven, whom He raised from the dead, that is Jesus, who rescues us from the wrath to come" (1Th. 1:2-10).

Chapter Five

Who Is Our Hope or Joy or Crown of Exultation

"But we, brethren, having been taken away from you for a short while — in person, not in spirit — were all the more eager with great desire to see your face. For we wanted to come to you — I, Paul, more than once — and yet Satan hindered us. For who is our hope or joy or crown of exultation? Is it not even you, in the presence of our Lord Jesus at His coming? For you are our glory and joy" (1Th. 2:17-20).

All the Joy with Which We Rejoice

"For this reason, when I could endure it no longer, I also sent to find out about your faith, for fear that the tempter might have tempted you, and our labor would be in vain. But now that Timothy has come to us from you, and has brought us good news of your faith and love, and that you always think kindly of us, longing to see us just as we also long to see you, for this reason, brethren, in all our distress and affliction we were comforted about you through your faith; for now we really live, if you stand firm in the Lord. For what thanks can we render to God for you in return for all the joy with which we rejoice before our God on your account, as we night and day keep praying most earnestly that we may see your face, and may complete what is lacking in your faith? Now may our God and Father Himself and Jesus our Lord direct our way to you" (1Th. 3:5-11).

Chapter Five

IN THE BOOK OF 2 TIMOTHY

So that I May Be Filled with Joy

"I thank God, whom I serve with a clear conscience the way my forefathers did, as I constantly remember you in my prayers night and day, longing to see you, even as I recall your tears, so that I may be filled with joy. For I am mindful of the sincere faith within you, which first dwelt in your grandmother Lois and your mother Eunice, and I am sure that it is in you as well. For this reason I remind you to kindle afresh the gift of God which is in you through the laying on of my hands. For God has not given us a spirit of timidity, but of power and love and discipline" (2Ti. 1:3-7).

IN THE BOOK OF PHILEMON

Much Joy and Comfort in Your Love

"I thank my God always, making mention of you in my prayers, because I hear of your love and of the faith which you have toward the Lord Jesus and toward all the saints; and I pray that the fellowship of your faith may become effective through the knowledge of every good thing which is in you for Christ's sake. For I have come to have much joy and comfort in your love, because the hearts of the saints have been refreshed through you, brother" (Phm. 1:4-7).

IN THE BOOK OF HEBREWS

For the Joy Set Before Him Endured the Cross

"Therefore, since we have so great a cloud of witnesses surrounding us, let us also lay aside every encumbrance and the sin which so easily entangles us, and let us run with endurance the race that is set before us, fixing our eyes on Jesus, the author and perfecter of faith, who for the joy set before Him endured the cross, despising the shame, and has sat down at the right hand of the throne of God" (Heb. 12:1-2).

With Joy and Not with Grief

"Obey your leaders and submit to them, for they keep watch over your souls as those who will give an account. Let them do this with joy and not with grief, for this would be unprofitable for you" (Heb. 13:17).

IN THE BOOK OF JAMES

Consider It All Joy, My Brethren

"Consider it all joy, my brethren, when you encounter various trials, knowing that the testing of your faith produces endurance. And let endurance have its perfect result, so that you may be perfect and complete, lacking in nothing". (Jas. 1:2-4).

Laughter Turned into Mourning and Your Joy to Gloom

"What is the source of quarrels and conflicts among you? Is not the source your pleasures that wage war in your members? You lust and do not have; so you commit murder. You are envious and cannot obtain; so you fight and quarrel. You do not have because you do not ask. You ask and do not receive, because you ask with wrong motives, so that you may spend it on your pleasures. You adulteresses, do you not know that friendship with the world is hostility toward God? Therefore whoever wishes to be a friend of the world makes himself an enemy of God. Or do you think that the Scripture speaks to no purpose: 'He jealously desires the Spirit which He has made to dwell in us'? But He gives a greater grace. Therefore it says, 'GOD IS OPPOSED TO THE PROUD, BUT GIVES GRACE TO THE HUMBLE.' Submit therefore to God. Resist the devil and he will flee from you. Draw near to God and He will draw near to you. Cleanse your hands, you sinners; and purify your hearts, you double-minded. Be miserable and mourn and weep; let your laughter be turned into mourning and your joy to gloom. Humble yourselves in the presence of the Lord, and He will exalt you" (Jas. 4:1-10).

Chapter Five

IN THE BOOK OF 1 PETER

Rejoice with Joy Inexpressible and Full of Glory

"Blessed be the God and Father of our Lord Jesus Christ, who according to His great mercy has caused us to be born again to a living hope through the resurrection of Jesus Christ from the dead, to obtain an inheritance which is imperishable and undefiled and will not fade away, reserved in heaven for you, who are protected by the power of God through faith for a salvation ready to be revealed in the last time. In this you greatly rejoice, even though now for a little while, if necessary, you have been distressed by various trials, so that the proof of your faith, being more precious than gold which is perishable, even though tested by fire, may be found to result in praise and glory and honor at the revelation of Jesus Christ; and though you have not seen Him, you love Him, and though you do not see Him now, but believe in Him, you greatly rejoice with joy inexpressible and full of glory, obtaining as the outcome of your faith the salvation of your souls" (1Pe. 1:3-9).

IN THE BOOK OF 1 JOHN

So that Our Joy May Be Made Complete

"What was from the beginning, what we have heard, what we have seen with our eyes, what we have looked at and touched with our hands, concerning the Word of Life — and the life was manifested, and we have seen and testify and proclaim to you the eternal life, which was with the Father and was manifested to us — what we have seen and heard we proclaim to you also, so that you too may have fellowship with us; and indeed our fellowship is with the Father, and with His Son Jesus Christ. These things we write, so that our joy may be made complete" (1Jn. 1:1-4).

IN THE BOOK OF 2 JOHN

So that Your Joy May Be Made Full

"Though I have many things to write to you, I do not want to do so with paper and ink; but I hope to come to you and speak face to face, so that your joy may be made full" (2Jn. 1:12).

IN THE BOOK OF 3 JOHN

I Have No Greater Joy than This

"Beloved, I pray that in all respects you may prosper and be in good health, just as your soul prospers. For I was very glad when brethren came and testified to your truth, that is, how you are walking in truth. I have no greater joy than this, to hear of my children walking in the truth" (3Jn. 1:2-4).

IN THE BOOK OF JUDE

Blameless with Great Joy

"Now to Him who is able to keep you from stumbling, and to make you stand in the presence of His glory blameless with great joy, to the only God our Savior, through Jesus Christ our Lord, be glory, majesty, dominion and authority, before all time and now and forever. Amen" (Jude 1:24-25).

RIGHTEOUS IN THE OLD TESTAMENT

IN THE BOOK OF GENESIS

Noah Was a Righteous Man, Blameless in His Time; Noah Walked with God.

"These are the records of the generations of Noah. Noah was a righteous man, blameless in his time; Noah walked with God. Noah became the father of three sons: Shem, Ham, and Japheth. Now the earth was corrupt in the sight of God, and the earth was filled with violence" (Ge. 6:9-11).

Will You Indeed Sweep Away the Righteous with the Wicked?

"Then the men turned away from there and went toward Sodom, while Abraham was still standing before the Lord. Abraham came near and said, 'Will You indeed sweep away the righteous with the wicked? Suppose there are fifty righteous within the city; will You indeed sweep it away and not spare the place for the sake of the fifty righteous who are in it? Far be it from You to do such a thing, to slay the righteous with the wicked, so that the righteous and the wicked are treated alike. Far be it from You! Shall not the Judge of all the earth deal justly?' So the Lord said, 'If I find in Sodom fifty righteous within the city, then I will spare the whole place on their account.' And Abraham replied, 'Now behold, I have ventured to speak to the Lord, although I am but dust and ashes. Suppose the fifty righteous are lacking five, will You destroy the whole city because of five?' And He said, 'I will not destroy it if I find forty-five there.' He spoke to Him yet again and said, 'Suppose forty are found there?' And He said, 'I will not do it on account of the forty.' Then he said, 'Oh may the Lord not be angry, and I shall speak; suppose thirty are found there?' And He said, 'I will not do it if I find thirty there.' And he said, 'Now behold, I have ventured to speak to the Lord; suppose twenty are found there?' And He said, 'I will not destroy it on account of the twenty.' Then he said, 'Oh may the Lord not be angry, and I shall speak only this once; suppose ten are found there?' And He said, 'I will not destroy it on account of the ten.' As soon as He had finished speaking to Abraham the Lord departed, and Abraham returned to his place" (Ge. 18:22-33).

IN THE BOOK OF DEUTERONOMY

A God of Faithfulness and Without Injustice, Righteous and Upright Is He

"Give ear, O heavens, and let me speak; and let the earth hear the words of my mouth. Let my teaching drop as the rain, my speech distill as the dew, as the droplets on the fresh grass and as the showers on the herb. For I proclaim the name of the Lord; ascribe greatness to our God! The Rock! His work is perfect, for all His ways are just; a God of faithfulness and without injustice, righteous and upright is He. They have acted corruptly toward Him, they are not His children, because of their defect; but are a perverse and crooked generation. Do you thus repay the Lord, O foolish and unwise people? Is not He your father who has bought you? He has made you and established you. Remember the days of old, consider the years of all generations. Ask your father, and he will inform you, your elders, and they will tell you. When the Most High gave the nations their inheritance, when He separated the sons of man, He set the boundaries of the peoples according to the number of the sons of Israel. For the Lord's portion is His people; Jacob is the allotment of His inheritance. He found him in a desert land, and in the howling waste of a wilderness; He encircled him, He cared for him, He guarded him as the pupil of His eye. Like an eagle that stirs up its nest, that hovers over its young, He spread His wings and caught them, He carried them on His pinions. The Lord alone guided him, and there was no foreign god with him. He made him ride on the high places of the earth, and he ate the produce of the field; and He made him suck honey from the rock, and oil from the flinty rock, curds of cows, and milk of the flock, with fat of lambs, and rams, the breed of Bashan, and goats, with the finest of the wheat—

and of the blood of grapes you drank wine" (De. 32:1-14).

IN THE BOOK OF PSALMS

The Lord Knows the Way of the Righteous

"The wicked are not so, but they are like chaff which the wind drives away. Therefore the wicked will not stand in the judgment, nor sinners in the assembly of the righteous. For the Lord knows the way of the righteous, but the way of the wicked will perish" (Ps. 1:4-6).

It Is You Who Blesses the Righteous Man, O Lord

"But let all who take refuge in You be glad, let them ever sing for joy; and may You shelter them, that those who love Your name may exult in You. For it is You who blesses the righteous man, O Lord, You surround him with favor as with a shield" (Ps. 5:11-12).

Establish the Righteous

"Arise, O Lord, in Your anger; lift up Yourself against the rage of my adversaries, and arouse Yourself for me; You have appointed judgment. Let the assembly of the peoples encompass You, and over them return on high. The Lord judges the peoples; vindicate me, O

Lord, according to my righteousness and my integrity that is in me. O let the evil of the wicked come to an end, but establish the righteous; for the righteous God tries the hearts and minds. My shield is with God, who saves the upright in heart. God is a righteous judge, and a God who has indignation every day" (Ps. 7:6-11).

If the Foundations Are Destroyed, What Can the Righteous Do?

"In the Lord I take refuge; how can you say to my soul, 'Flee as a bird to your mountain; for, behold, the wicked bend the bow, they make ready their arrow upon the string to shoot in darkness at the upright in heart. If the foundations are destroyed, what can the righteous do" (Ps. 11:1-3)?

The Lord Tests the Righteous and the Wicked

"The Lord is in His holy temple; the Lord's throne is in heaven; His eyes behold, His eyelids test the sons of men. The Lord tests the righteous and the wicked, and the one who loves violence His soul hates. Upon the wicked He will rain snares; fire and brimstone and burning wind will be the portion of their cup. For the Lord is righteous, He loves righteousness; the upright will behold His face" (Ps. 11:4-7).

Chapter Six

The Judgments of the Lord Are True; They Are Righteous Altogether

"The law of the Lord is perfect, restoring the soul; the testimony of the Lord is sure, making wise the simple. The precepts of the Lord are right, rejoicing the heart; the commandment of the Lord is pure, enlightening the eyes. The fear of the Lord is clean, enduring forever; the judgments of the Lord are true; they are righteous altogether. They are more desirable than gold, yes, than much fine gold; sweeter also than honey and the drippings of the honeycomb. Moreover, by them Your servant is warned; in keeping them there is great reward. Who can discern his errors? Acquit me of hidden faults. Also keep back Your servant from presumptuous sins; let them not rule over me; then I will be blameless, and I shall be acquitted of great transgression. Let the words of my mouth and the meditation of my heart Be acceptable in Your sight, O Lord, my rock and my Redeemer" (Ps. 19:7-14).

Be Glad in the Lord and Rejoice, You Righteous Ones

"I will instruct you and teach you in the way which you should go; I will counsel you with My eye upon you. Do not be as the horse or as the mule which have no understanding, whose trappings include bit and bridle to hold them in check, otherwise they will not come near to you.

Many are the sorrows of the wicked, but he who trusts in the Lord, lovingkindness shall surround him. Be glad in the Lord and rejoice, you righteous ones; and shout for joy, all you who are upright in heart" (Ps. 32:8-11).

The Eyes of the Lord Are Toward the Righteous

"The eyes of the Lord are toward the righteous and His ears are open to their cry. The face of the Lord is against evildoers, to cut off the memory of them from the earth. The righteous cry, and the Lord hears and delivers them out of all their troubles. The Lord is near to the brokenhearted and saves those who are crushed in spirit" (Ps. 34:15-18).

The Righteous Cry, and the Lord Hears

"The eyes of the Lord are toward the righteous and His ears are open to their cry. The face of the Lord is against evildoers, to cut off the memory of them from the earth. The righteous cry, and the Lord hears and delivers them out of all their troubles. The Lord is near to the brokenhearted and saves those who are crushed in spirit" (Ps. 34:15-18).

Many Are the Afflictions of the Righteous

"Many are the afflictions of the righteous, but the Lord delivers him out of them all. He keeps all his bones, not one of them is broken. Evil shall slay the wicked, and those who hate the righteous will be condemned. The Lord redeems the soul of His servants, and none of those who take refuge in Him will be condemned" (Ps. 34:19-22).

The Wicked Plots Against the Righteous

"The wicked plots against the righteous and gnashes at him with his teeth. The Lord laughs at him, for He sees his day is coming. The wicked have drawn the sword and bent their bow to cast down the afflicted and the needy, to slay those who are upright in conduct. Their sword will enter their own heart, and their bows will be broken" (Ps. 37:12-15).

The Lord Sustains the Righteous

"Better is the little of the righteous than the abundance of many wicked. For the arms of the wicked will be broken, but the Lord sustains the righteous. The Lord knows the days of the blameless, and their inheritance will be forever. They will not be ashamed in the time of evil, and in the days of famine they will have abundance. But the wicked will perish; and the enemies of the Lord will be like the glory of the pastures, they vanish—like smoke they vanish away. The wicked borrows and does not pay back, but the righteous is gracious and gives. For those blessed by Him will inherit the land, but those cursed by Him will be cut off" (Ps. 37:16-22).

I Have Not Seen the Righteous Forsaken

"The steps of a man are established by the Lord, and He delights in his way. When he falls, he will not be hurled headlong, because the Lord is the One who holds his hand. I have been young and now I am old, yet I have not seen the righteous forsaken or his descendants begging bread. All day long he is gracious and lends, and his descendants are a blessing" (Ps. 37:23-26).

The Mouth of the Righteous Utters Wisdom

"Depart from evil and do good, so you will abide forever. For the Lord loves justice and does not forsake His godly ones; they are preserved forever, but the descendants of the wicked will be cut off. The righteous will inherit the land and dwell in it forever. The mouth of the righteous utters wisdom, and his tongue speaks justice. The law of his God is in his heart; His steps do not slip. The wicked spies upon the righteous and seeks to kill him. The Lord will not leave him in his hand or let him be condemned when he is judged. Wait for the Lord and keep His way, and He will exalt you to inherit the land; when the wicked are cut off, you will see it" (Ps. 37:27-34).

The Salvation of the Righteous Is from the Lord

"I have seen a wicked, violent man spreading himself like a luxuriant tree in its native soil. Then he passed away, and lo, he was no more; I sought for him, but he could not be found. Mark the blameless man, and behold the upright; for the man of peace will have a posterity. But transgressors will be altogether destroyed; the posterity of the wicked will be cut off. But the salvation of the righteous is from the Lord; He is their strength in time of trouble. The Lord helps them and delivers them; He delivers them from the wicked and saves them, because they take refuge in Him" (Ps. 37:35-40).

He Will Never Allow the Righteous to Be Shaken

"Cast your burden upon the Lord and He will sustain you; He will never allow the righteous to be shaken. But You, O God, will bring them down to the pit of destruction; men of bloodshed and deceit will not live out half their days. But I will trust in You" (Ps. 55:22-23).

The Righteous Will Rejoice when He Sees the Vengeance

"The righteous will rejoice when he sees the vengeance; he will wash his feet in the blood of the wicked. And men will say, 'Surely there is a reward for the righteous; surely there is a God who judges on earth"' (Ps. 58:10-11)!

The Righteous Man Will Be Glad in the Lord and Will Take Refuge in Him

"Hear my voice, O God, in my complaint; preserve my life from dread of the enemy. Hide me from the secret counsel of evildoers, from the tumult of those who do iniquity, who have sharpened their tongue like a sword. They aimed bitter speech as their arrow, to shoot from concealment at the blameless; suddenly they shoot at him, and do not fear. They hold fast to themselves an evil purpose; they talk of laying snares secretly; they say, 'Who can see them?' They devise injustices, saying, 'We are ready with a well-conceived plot'; for the inward thought and the heart of a man are deep. But God will shoot at them with an arrow; suddenly they will be wounded. So they will make him stumble; their own tongue is against them; all who see them will shake the head. Then all men will fear, and they will declare the work of God, and will consider what He has done. The righteous man will be glad in the Lord and will take refuge in Him; and all the upright in heart will glory" (Ps. 64:1-10).

The Righteous Flourish

"Let them fear You while the sun endures, and as long as the moon, throughout all generations. May he come down like rain upon the mown grass, like showers that water the earth. In his days may the righteous flourish, and abundance of peace till the moon is no more" (Ps. 72:5-7).

The Horns of the Righteous Will Be Lifted Up

"For not from the east, nor from the west, nor from the desert comes exaltation; but God is the Judge; He puts down one and exalts another. For a cup is in the hand of the Lord, and the wine foams; it is well mixed, and He pours out of this; surely all the wicked of the earth must drain and drink down its dregs. But as for me, I will declare it forever; I will sing praises to the God of Jacob. And all the horns of the wicked He will cut off, but the horns of the righteous will be lifted up" (Ps. 75:6-10).

The Righteous Man Will Flourish Like the Palm Tree

"But You have exalted my horn like that of the wild ox; I have been anointed with fresh oil. And my eye has looked exultantly upon my foes, my ears hear of the evildoers who rise up against me. The righteous man will flourish like the palm tree, he will grow like a cedar in Lebanon. Planted in the house of the Lord, they will flourish in the courts of our God. They will still yield fruit in old age; they shall be full of sap and very green, to declare that the Lord is upright; he is my rock, and there is no unrighteousness in Him" (Ps. 92:10-15).

They Band Themselves Together Against the Life of the Righteous

"If the Lord had not been my help, my soul would soon have dwelt in the abode of silence. If I should say, 'My foot has slipped,' Your lovingkindness, O Lord, will hold me up. When my anxious thoughts multiply within me, Your consolations delight my soul. Can a throne of destruction be allied with You, one which devises mischief by decree? They band themselves together against the life of the righteous and condemn the innocent to death. But the Lord has been my stronghold, and my God the rock of my refuge. He has brought back their wickedness upon them and will destroy them in their evil; the Lord our God will destroy them" (Ps. 94:17-23).

Light Is Sown Like Seed for the Righteous

"Hate evil, you who love the Lord, who preserves the souls of His godly ones; He delivers them from the hand of the wicked. Light is sown like seed for the righteous and gladness for the upright in heart. Be glad in the Lord, you righteous ones, and give thanks to His holy name" (Ps. 97:10-12).

The Lord Performs Righteous Deeds

"The Lord performs righteous deeds and judgments for all who are oppressed. He made known His ways to Moses, His acts to the sons of Israel. The Lord is compassionate and gracious, slow to anger and abounding in lovingkindness. He will not always strive with us, nor will He keep His anger forever. He has not dealt with us according to our sins, nor rewarded us according to our iniquities. For as high as the heavens are above the earth, so great is His lovingkindness toward those who fear Him. As far as the east is from the west, so far has He removed our transgressions from us. Just as a father has compassion on his children, so the Lord has compassion on those who fear Him. For He Himself knows our frame; He is mindful that we are but dust" (Ps. 103:6-14).

He Is Gracious and Compassionate and Righteous

"Praise the Lord! How blessed is the man who fears the Lord, who greatly delights in His commandments. His descendants will be mighty on earth; the generation of the upright will be blessed. Wealth and riches are in his house, and his righteousness endures forever. Light arises in the darkness for the upright; He is gracious and compassionate and righteous. It is well with the man who is gracious and lends; He will maintain his cause in judgment. For he will never be shaken; the righteous will be remembered forever" (Ps. 112:1-6).

Gracious Is the Lord, and Righteous

"Gracious is the Lord, and righteous; yes, our God is compassionate. The Lord preserves the simple; I was brought low, and He saved me. Return to your rest, O my soul, for the Lord has dealt bountifully with you. For You have rescued my soul from death, my eyes from tears, my feet from stumbling. I shall walk before the Lord in the land of the living. I believed when I said, 'I am greatly afflicted.' I said in my alarm, 'All men are liars'" (Ps. 116:5-11).

Joyful Shouting and Salvation Is in the Tents of the Righteous

"The sound of joyful shouting and salvation is in the tents of the righteous; the right hand of the Lord does valiantly. The right hand of the Lord is exalted; the right hand of the Lord does valiantly. I will not die, but live, and tell of the works of the Lord. The Lord has disciplined me severely, but He has not given me over to death" (Ps. 118:15-18).

The Righteous Will Enter Through It

"Open to me the gates of righteousness; I shall enter through them, I shall give thanks to the Lord. This is the gate of the Lord; the righteous will enter through it. I shall give thanks to You, for You have answered me, and You have become my salvation" (Ps. 118:19-21).

I Learn Your Righteous Judgments

"How blessed are those whose way is blameless, who walk in the law of the Lord. How blessed are those who observe His testimonies, who seek Him with all their heart. They also do no unrighteousness; they walk in His ways. You have ordained Your precepts, that we should keep them diligently. Oh that my ways may be established to keep Your statutes! Then I shall not be ashamed when I look upon all Your commandments. I shall give thanks to You with uprightness of heart, when I learn Your righteous judgments. I shall keep Your statutes; do not forsake me utterly" (Ps. 119:1-8)!

Because of Your Righteous Ordinances

"The Lord is my portion; I have promised to keep Your words. I sought Your favor with all my heart; be gracious to me according to Your word. I considered my ways and turned my feet to Your testimonies. I hastened and did not delay to keep Your commandments. The cords of the wicked have encircled me, but I have not forgotten Your law. At midnight I shall rise to give thanks to You because of Your righteous ordinances. I am a companion of all those who fear You, and of those who keep Your precepts. The earth is full of Your lovingkindness, O Lord; teach me Your statutes" (Ps. 119:57-64).

O Lord, that Your Judgments Are Righteous

"Your hands made me and fashioned me; give me understanding, that I may learn Your commandments. May those who fear You see me and be glad, because I wait for Your word. I know, O Lord, that Your judgments are righteous, and that in faithfulness You have afflicted me. O may Your lovingkindness comfort me, according to Your word to Your servant. May Your compassion come to me that I may live, for Your law is my delight. May the arrogant be ashamed, for they subvert me with a lie; but I shall meditate on Your precepts. May those who fear You turn to me, even those who know Your testimonies. May my heart be blameless in Your statutes, so that I will not be ashamed" (Ps. 119:73-80).

I Will Keep Your Righteous Ordinances

"Your word is a lamp to my feet and a light to my path. I have sworn and I will confirm it, that I will keep Your righteous ordinances. I am exceedingly afflicted; revive me, O Lord, according to Your word. O accept the freewill offerings of my mouth, O Lord, and teach me Your ordinances. My life is continually in my hand, yet I do not forget Your law. The wicked have laid a snare for me, yet I have not gone astray from Your precepts. I have inherited Your testimonies forever, for they are the joy of my heart. I have inclined my heart to perform Your statutes forever, even to the end" (Ps. 119:105-112).

Your Righteous Word

"I have done justice and righteousness; do not leave me to my oppressors. Be surety for Your servant for good; do not let the arrogant oppress me. My eyes fail with longing for Your salvation and for Your righteous word. Deal with Your servant according to Your lovingkindness and teach me Your statutes. I am Your servant; give me understanding, that I may know Your testimonies. It is time for the Lord to act, for they have broken Your law. Therefore I love Your commandments above gold, yes, above fine gold. Therefore I esteem right all Your precepts concerning everything, I hate every false way" (Ps. 119:121-128).

Righteous Are You, O Lord

"Righteous are You, O Lord, and upright are Your judgments. You have commanded Your testimonies in righteousness and exceeding faithfulness. My zeal has consumed me, because my adversaries have forgotten Your words. Your word is very pure, therefore Your servant loves it. I am small and despised, yet I do not forget Your precepts. Your righteousness is an everlasting righteousness, and Your law is truth. Trouble and anguish have come upon me, yet Your commandments are my delight. Your testimonies are righteous forever; give me understanding that I may live" (Ps. 119:137-144).

Every One of Your Righteous Ordinances Is Everlasting

"Look upon my affliction and rescue me, for I do not forget Your law. Plead my cause and redeem me; revive me according to Your word. Salvation is far from the wicked, for they do not seek Your statutes. Great are Your mercies, O Lord; revive me according to Your ordinances. Many are my persecutors and my adversaries, yet I do not turn aside from Your testimonies. I behold the treacherous and loathe them, because they do not keep Your word. Consider how I love Your precepts; revive me, O Lord, according to Your lovingkindness. The sum of Your word is truth, and every one of Your righteous ordinances is everlasting" (Ps. 119:153-160).

Chapter Six

Because of Your Righteous Ordinances

"Princes persecute me without cause, but my heart stands in awe of Your words. I rejoice at Your word, as one who finds great spoil. I hate and despise falsehood, but I love Your law. Seven times a day I praise You, because of Your righteous ordinances. Those who love Your law have great peace, and nothing causes them to stumble. I hope for Your salvation, O Lord, and do Your commandments. My soul keeps Your testimonies, and I love them exceedingly. I keep Your precepts and Your testimonies, for all my ways are before You" (Ps. 119:161-168).

Upon the Land of the Righteous

"Those who trust in the Lord are as Mount Zion, which cannot be moved but abides forever. As the mountains surround Jerusalem, so the Lord surrounds His people from this time forth and forever. For the scepter of wickedness shall not rest upon the land of the righteous, so that the righteous will not put forth their hands to do wrong" (Ps. 125:1-3).

The Lord Is Righteous; He Has Cut in Two the Cords of the Wicked

"'Many times they have persecuted me from my youth up,' let Israel now say, 'Many times they have persecuted me from my youth up;

yet they have not prevailed against me. The plowers plowed upon my back; they lengthened their furrows.' The Lord is righteous; He has cut in two the cords of the wicked" (Ps. 129:1-4).

Surely the Righteous Will Give Thanks to Your Name

"I know that the Lord will maintain the cause of the afflicted and justice for the poor. Surely the righteous will give thanks to Your name; the upright will dwell in Your presence" (Ps. 140:12-13).

The Righteous

"Let the righteous smite me in kindness and reprove me; it is oil upon the head; do not let my head refuse it, for still my prayer is against their wicked deeds. Their judges are thrown down by the sides of the rock, and they hear my words, for they are pleasant. As when one plows and breaks open the earth, our bones have been scattered at the mouth of Sheol" (Ps. 141:5-7).

The Righteous Will Surround Me, for You Will Deal Bountifully with Me

"I cried out to You, O Lord; I said, 'You are my refuge, my portion in the land of the living. Give heed to my cry, for I am brought very low; deliver me from my persecutors, for they are too strong for me. Bring my soul out of prison, so that I may give thanks to Your name; the righteous will surround me, for You will deal bountifully with me" (Ps. 142:5-7).

The Lord is Righteous in All His Ways

"The Lord is righteous in all His ways and kind in all His deeds. The Lord is near to all who call upon Him, to all who call upon Him in truth. He will fulfill the desire of those who fear Him; He will also hear their cry and will save them. The Lord keeps all who love Him, but all the wicked He will destroy. My mouth will speak the praise of the Lord, and all flesh will bless His holy name forever and ever" (Ps. 145:17-21).

The Lord Loves the Righteous

"The Lord opens the eyes of the blind; the Lord raises up those who are bowed down; the Lord loves the righteous; the Lord protects the strangers; He supports the fatherless and the widow, but He thwarts the way of the wicked. The Lord will reign forever, your God, O Zion, to all generations. Praise the Lord" (Ps. 146:8-10)!

IN THE BOOK OF PROVERBS

I will not give titles to these verses because they are small; however, I would like to say something additional. The "fear of the Lord" is the theme that can be found in the book of Proverbs. "The connection between the promise and wisdom was the same as the connection between the law and the promise. Wisdom frequently took the instruction given in Torah and popularized it by placing it in proverbial forms that were brief, memorable, and with a bit of a salty edge that condensed the command into a witticism that could be carried in their memory."[4]

"The curse of the Lord is on the house of the wicked, but He blesses the dwelling of the righteous" (Pr. 3:33).

"But the path of the righteous is like the light of dawn, that shines brighter and brighter until the full day" (Pr. 4:18).

"Give instruction to a wise man and he will be still wiser, teach a righteous man and he will increase his learning" (Pr. 9:9).

"The Lord will not allow the righteous to hunger, but He will reject the craving of the wicked" (Pr. 10:3).

"Blessings are on the head of the righteous, but the mouth of the wicked conceals violence" (Pr. 10:6).

---

[4] Walter C. Kaiser Jr., *The Promise Plan of God*, Zondervan, Grand Rapids, 1978, 150.

"The memory of the righteous is blessed, but the name of the wicked will rot" (Pr. 10:7).

"The mouth of the righteous is a fountain of life, but the mouth of the wicked conceals violence" (Pr. 10:11).

"The wages of the righteous is life, the income of the wicked, punishment" (Pr. 10:16).

"The tongue of the righteous is as choice silver, the heart of the wicked is worth little" (Pr. 10:20).

"The lips of the righteous feed many, but fools die for lack of understanding" (Pr. 10:21).

"What the wicked fears will come upon him, but the desire of the righteous will be granted" (Pr. 10:24).

"When the whirlwind passes, the wicked is no more, but the righteous has an everlasting foundation" (Pr. 10:25).

"The hope of the righteous is gladness, but the expectation of the wicked perishes" (Pr. 10:28).

"The righteous will never be shaken, but the wicked will not dwell in the land" (Pr. 10:30).

"The mouth of the righteous flows with wisdom, but the perverted tongue will be cut out" (Pr.

10:31).

"The lips of the righteous bring forth what is acceptable, but the mouth of the wicked what is perverted" (Pr. 10:32).

"The righteous is delivered from trouble, but the wicked takes his place" (Pr. 11:8).

"With his mouth the godless man destroys his neighbor, but through knowledge the righteous will be delivered" (Pr. 11:9).

"When it goes well with the righteous, the city rejoices, and when the wicked perish, there is joyful shouting" (Pr. 11:10).

"Assuredly, the evil man will not go unpunished, but the descendants of the righteous will be delivered" (Pr. 11:21).

"The desire of the righteous is only good, but the expectation of the wicked is wrath" (Pr. 11:23).

"He who trusts in his riches will fall, but the righteous will flourish like the green leaf" (Pr. 11:28).

"The fruit of the righteous is a tree of life, and he who is wise wins souls" (Pr. 11:30).

"If the righteous will be rewarded in the earth,

how much more the wicked and the sinner" (Pr. 11:31)!

"A man will not be established by wickedness, but the root of the righteous will not be moved" (Pr. 12:3).

"The thoughts of the righteous are just, but the counsels of the wicked are deceitful" (Pr. 12:5).

"The wicked are overthrown and are no more, but the house of the righteous will stand" (Pr. 12:7).

"A righteous man has regard for the life of his animal, but even the compassion of the wicked is cruel" (Pr. 12:10).

"The wicked man desires the booty of evil men, but the root of the righteous yields fruit" (Pr. 12:12).

"An evil man is ensnared by the transgression of his lips, but the righteous will escape from trouble" (Pr. 12:13).

"No harm befalls the righteous, but the wicked are filled with trouble" (Pr. 12:21).
"The righteous is a guide to his neighbor, but the way of the wicked leads them astray" (Pr. 12:26).

"A righteous man hates falsehood, but a wicked man acts disgustingly and shamefully" (Pr. 13:5).

"The light of the righteous rejoices, but the lamp of the wicked goes out" (Pr. 13:9).

"Adversity pursues sinners, but the righteous will be rewarded with prosperity" (Pr. 13:21).

"A good man leaves an inheritance to his children's children, and the wealth of the sinner is stored up for the righteous" (Pr. 13:22).

"The righteous has enough to satisfy his appetite, but the stomach of the wicked is in need" (Pr. 13:25).

"The evil will bow down before the good, and the wicked at the gates of the righteous" (Pr. 14:19).

"The wicked is thrust down by his wrongdoing, but the righteous has a refuge when he dies" (Pr. 14:32).

"Great wealth is in the house of the righteous, but trouble is in the income of the wicked" (Pr. 15:6).

"The heart of the righteous ponders how to answer, but the mouth of the wicked pours out evil things" (Pr. 15:28).

"The Lord is far from the wicked, but He hears the prayer of the righteous" (Pr. 15:29).

"Righteous lips are the delight of kings, and he who speaks right is loved" (Pr. 16:13).

"He who justifies the wicked and he who condemns the righteous, both of them alike are an abomination to the Lord" (Pr. 17:15).

"It is also not good to fine the righteous, nor to strike the noble for their uprightness" (Pr. 17:26).

"To show partiality to the wicked is not good, nor to thrust aside the righteous in judgment" (Pr. 18:5).

"The name of the Lord is a strong tower; the righteous runs into it and is safe" (Pr. 18:10).

"A righteous man who walks in his integrity how blessed are his sons after him" (Pr. 20:7).
"The righteous one considers the house of the wicked, turning the wicked to ruin" (Pr. 21:12).

"The exercise of justice is joy for the righteous, but is terror to the workers of iniquity" (Pr. 21:15).

"The wicked is a ransom for the righteous, and the treacherous is in the place of the upright" (Pr. 21:18).

"All day long he is craving, while the righteous gives and does not hold back" (Pr. 21:26).

"The father of the righteous will greatly rejoice, and he who sires a wise son will be glad in him" (Pr. 23:24).

"Do not lie in wait, O wicked man, against the dwelling of the righteous; Do not destroy his resting place; Pr 24:15

"For a righteous man falls seven times, and rises again, but the wicked stumble in time of calamity" (Pr. 24:16).

"He who says to the wicked, 'You are righteous,' peoples will curse him, nations will abhor him" (Pr. 24:24).

"Like a trampled spring and a polluted well is a righteous man who gives way before the wicked" (Pr. 25:26).

"The wicked flee when no one is pursuing, but the righteous are bold as a lion" (Pr. 28:1).

"When the righteous triumph, there is great glory, but when the wicked rise, men hide themselves" (Pr. 28:12).

"When the wicked rise, men hide themselves; but when they perish, the righteous increase" (Pr. 28:28).

"When the righteous increase, the people rejoice, but when a wicked man rules, people groan" (Pr. 29:2).

"By transgression an evil man is ensnared, but the righteous sings and rejoices" (Pr. 29:6).

"The righteous is concerned for the rights of the poor, the wicked does not understand such concern" (Pr. 29:7).

"When the wicked increase, transgression increases; but the righteous will see their fall" (Pr. 29:16).

"An unjust man is abominable to the righteous, and he who is upright in the way is abominable to the wicked" (Pr. 29:27).

Chapter Seven

RIGHTEOUS IN THE NEW TESTAMENT

IN THE BOOK OF MARK

I Did Not Come to Call the Righteous, but Sinners

"And it happened that He was reclining at the table in his house, and many tax collectors and sinners were dining with Jesus and His disciples; for there were many of them, and they were following Him. When the scribes of the Pharisees saw that He was eating with the sinners and tax collectors, they said to His disciples, 'Why is He eating and drinking with tax collectors and sinners?' And hearing this, Jesus said to them, 'It is not those who are healthy who need a physician, but those who are sick; I did not come to call the righteous, but sinners'" (Mr. 2:15-17).

Knowing that He Was a Righteous and Holy Man

"For Herod himself had sent and had John arrested and bound in prison on account of Herodias, the wife of his brother Philip, because he had married her. For John had been saying to Herod, 'It is not lawful for you to have your brother's wife.' Herodias had a grudge against him and wanted to put him to death and could not do so; for Herod was afraid of John, knowing that he was a righteous and holy man, and he kept him safe. And when he heard him, he was very perplexed; but he used to enjoy listening to him. A strategic day came when Herod on his birthday gave a banquet for his lords and military commanders and the leading men of Galilee; and when the daughter of Herodias herself came in and danced, she pleased Herod and his dinner guests; and the king said to the girl, 'Ask me for whatever you want and I will give it to you.' And he swore to her, 'Whatever you ask of me, I will give it to you; up to half of my kingdom.' And she went out and said to her mother, 'What shall I ask for?' And she said, 'The head of John the Baptist.' Immediately she came in a hurry to the king and asked, saying, 'I want you to give me at once the head of John the Baptist on a platter.' And although the king was very sorry, yet because of his oaths and because of his dinner guests, he was unwilling to refuse her. Immediately the king sent an executioner and commanded him to bring back his head. And he went and had him beheaded in the prison, and brought his head on a platter, and gave it to the girl; and the girl gave it to her mother. When his disciples heard about this, they came and took away his body and laid it in a tomb" (Mr. 6:17-29).

Chapter Seven

IN THE BOOK OF LUKE

They Were Both Righteous in the Sight of God, Walking Blamelessly

"In the days of Herod, king of Judea, there was a priest named Zacharias, of the division of Abijah; and he had a wife from the daughters of Aaron, and her name was Elizabeth. They were both righteous in the sight of God, walking blamelessly in all the commandments and requirements of the Lord. But they had no child, because Elizabeth was barren, and they were both advanced in years" (Lu. 1:5-7).

The Disobedient to the Attitude of the Righteous

"Now it happened that while he was performing his priestly service before God in the appointed order of his division, according to the custom of the priestly office, he was chosen by lot to enter the temple of the Lord and burn incense. And the whole multitude of the people were in prayer outside at the hour of the incense offering. And an angel of the Lord appeared to him, standing to the right of the altar of incense. Zacharias was troubled when he saw the angel, and fear gripped him. But the angel said to him, 'Do not be afraid, Zacharias, for your petition has been heard, and your wife Elizabeth will bear you a son, and you will give him the name John. You will have joy and gladness, and many will rejoice at his birth. For he will be great in the sight of the Lord; and he will drink no wine or liquor, and he will be filled with the Holy Spirit while yet in his mother's womb. And he will turn many of the sons of Israel back to the Lord their God. It is he who will go as a forerunner before Him in the spirit and power of Elijah, TO TURN THE HEARTS OF THE FATHERS BACK TO THE CHILDREN, and the disobedient to the attitude of the righteous, so as to make ready a people prepared for the Lord'" (Lu. 1:8-17).

This Man Was Righteous and Devout

"And there was a man in Jerusalem whose name was Simeon; and this man was righteous and devout, looking for the consolation of Israel; and the Holy Spirit was upon him. And it had been revealed to him by the Holy Spirit that he would not see death before he had seen the Lord's Christ. And he came in the Spirit into the temple; and when the parents brought in the child Jesus, to carry out for Him the custom of the Law, then he took Him into his arms, and blessed God, and said, 'Now Lord, You are releasing Your bond-servant to depart in peace, according to Your word; for my eyes have seen Your salvation, which You have prepared in the presence of all peoples, A LIGHT OF REVELATION TO THE GENTILES, and the glory of Your people Israel'" (Lu. 2:25-32).

I Have Not Come to Call the Righteous but Sinners to Repentance

"And Levi gave a big reception for Him in his house; and there was a great crowd of tax collectors and other people who were reclining at the table with them. The Pharisees and their scribes began grumbling at His disciples, saying, 'Why do you eat and drink with the tax collectors and sinners?' And Jesus answered and said to them, 'It is not those who are well who need a physician, but those who are sick. I have not come to call the righteous but sinners to repentance'" (Lu. 5:29-32).

You Will Be Repaid at the Resurrection of the Righteous

"And He also went on to say to the one who had invited Him, 'When you give a luncheon or a dinner, do not invite your friends or your brothers or your relatives or rich neighbors, otherwise they may also invite you in return and that will be your repayment. But when you give a reception, invite the poor, the crippled, the lame, the blind, and you will be blessed, since they do not have the means to repay you; for you will be repaid at the resurrection of the righteous'" (Lu. 14:12-14).

Ninety-Nine Righteous

"So He told them this parable, saying, 'What man among you, if he has a hundred sheep and has lost one of them, does not leave the ninety-nine in the open pasture and go after the one which is lost until he finds it? When he has found it, he lays it on his shoulders, rejoicing. And when he comes home, he calls together his friends and his neighbors, saying to them, "Rejoice with me, for I have found my sheep which was lost!" I tell you that in the same way, there will be more joy in heaven over one sinner who repents than over ninety-nine righteous persons who need no repentance'" (Lu. 15:3-7).

Spies Who Pretended to Be Righteous

"The scribes and the chief priests tried to lay hands on Him that very hour, and they feared the people; for they understood that He spoke this parable against them. So they watched Him, and sent spies who pretended to be righteous, in order that they might catch Him in some statement, so that they could deliver Him to the rule and the authority of the governor. They questioned Him, saying, 'Teacher, we know that You speak and teach correctly, and You are not partial to any, but teach the way of God in truth. Is it lawful for us to pay taxes to Caesar, or not?' But He detected their trickery and said to them, 'Show Me a denarius. Whose likeness and inscription does it have?'

They said, 'Caesar's.' And He said to them, 'Then render to Caesar the things that are Caesar's, and to God the things that are God's.' And they were unable to catch Him in a saying in the presence of the people; and being amazed at His answer, they became silent" (Lu. 20:19-26).

A Good and Righteous Man

"And a man named Joseph, who was a member of the Council, a good and righteous man (he had not consented to their plan and action), a man from Arimathea, a city of the Jews, who was waiting for the kingdom of God; this man went to Pilate and asked for the body of Jesus. And he took it down and wrapped it in a linen cloth, and laid Him in a tomb cut into the rock, where no one had ever lain. It was the preparation day, and the Sabbath was about to begin. Now the women who had come with Him out of Galilee followed, and saw the tomb and how His body was laid. Then they returned and prepared spices and perfumes. And on the Sabbath they rested according to the commandment" (Lu. 23:50-56).

IN THE BOOK OF JOHN

Judge with Righteous Judgment

"'Did not Moses give you the Law, and yet none of you carries out the Law? Why do you seek to kill Me?' The crowd answered, 'You have a demon! Who seeks to kill You?' Jesus answered them, 'I did one deed, and you all marvel. For this reason Moses has given you circumcision (not because it is from Moses, but from the fathers), and on the Sabbath you circumcise a man. If a man receives circumcision on the Sabbath so that the Law of Moses will not be broken, are you angry with Me because I made an entire man well on the Sabbath? Do not judge according to appearance, but judge with righteous judgment'" (Jn. 7:19-24).

O Righteous Father

"O righteous Father, although the world has not known You, yet I have known You; and these have known that You sent Me; and I have made Your name known to them, and will make it known, so that the love with which You loved Me may be in them, and I in them" (Jn. 17:25-26).

IN THE BOOK OF ACTS

You Disowned the Holy and Righteous One and Asked for a Murderer

"While he was clinging to Peter and John, all the people ran together to them at the so-called portico of Solomon, full of amazement. But when Peter saw this, he replied to the people, 'Men of Israel, why are you amazed at this, or why do you gaze at us, as if by our own power or piety we had made him walk? The God of Abraham, Isaac and

Jacob, the God of our fathers, has glorified His servant Jesus, the one whom you delivered and disowned in the presence of Pilate, when he had decided to release Him. But you disowned the Holy and Righteous One and asked for a murderer to be granted to you, but put to death the Prince of life, the one whom God raised from the dead, a fact to which we are witnesses. And on the basis of faith in His name, it is the name of Jesus which has strengthened this man whom you see and know; and the faith which comes through Him has given him this perfect health in the presence of you all'" (Ac. 3:11-16).

Previously Announced the Coming of the Righteous One

"You men who are stiff-necked and uncircumcised in heart and ears are always resisting the Holy Spirit; you are doing just as your fathers did. Which one of the prophets did your fathers not persecute? They killed those who had previously announced the coming of the Righteous One, whose betrayers and murderers you have now become; you who received the law as ordained by angels, and yet did not keep it" (Ac. 7:51-53).

A Centurion, a Righteous and God-Fearing Man

"Now while Peter was greatly perplexed in mind as to what the vision which he had seen might be, behold, the men who had been sent by Cornelius, having asked directions for Simon's house, appeared at the gate; and calling out, they were asking whether Simon, who was also called Peter, was staying there. While Peter was reflecting on the vision, the Spirit said to him, 'Behold, three men are looking for you. But get up, go downstairs and accompany them without misgivings, for I have sent them Myself.' Peter went down to the men and said, 'Behold, I am the one you are looking for; what is the reason for which you have come?' They said, 'Cornelius, a centurion, a righteous and God-fearing man well spoken of by the entire nation of the Jews, was divinely directed by a holy angel to send for you to come to his house and hear a message from you.' So he invited them in and gave them lodging. And on the next day he got up and went away with them, and some of the brethren from Joppa accompanied him. On the following day he entered Caesarea. Now Cornelius was waiting for them and had called together his relatives and close friends. When Peter entered, Cornelius met him, and fell at his feet and worshiped him. But Peter raised him up, saying, 'Stand up; I too am just a man.' As he talked with him, he entered and *found many people assembled. And he said to them, 'You yourselves know how unlawful it is for a man who is a Jew to associate with a foreigner or to visit him; and yet God has shown me that I should not call any man unholy or unclean. That is why I came without even raising any objection when I was sent for. So I ask for what reason you have sent for me'" (Ac. 10:17-29).

The Righteous One

"A certain Ananias, a man who was devout by the standard of the Law, and well spoken of by all the Jews who lived there, came to me, and standing near said to me, 'Brother Saul, receive your sight!' And at that very time I looked up at him. And he said, 'The God of our fathers has appointed you to know His will and to see the Righteous One and to hear an utterance from His mouth. For you will be a witness for Him to all men of what you have seen and heard. Now why do you delay? Get up and be baptized, and wash away your sins, calling on His name'" (Ac. 22:12-16).

Both the Righteous and the Wicked

"When the governor had nodded for him to speak, Paul responded: 'Knowing that for many years you have been a judge to this nation, I cheerfully make my defense, since you can take note of the fact that no more than twelve days ago I went up to Jerusalem to worship. Neither in the temple, nor in the synagogues, nor in the city itself did they find me carrying on a discussion with anyone or causing a riot. Nor can they prove to you the charges of which they now accuse me. But this I admit to you, that according to the Way which they call a sect I do serve the God of our fathers, believing everything that is in accordance with the Law and that is written in the Prophets; having a hope in God, which these men cherish themselves, that there shall certainly be a resurrection of both the righteous and the wicked. In view of this, I also do my best to maintain always a blameless conscience both before God and before men. Now after several years I came to bring alms to my nation and to present offerings; in which they found me occupied in the temple, having been purified, without any crowd or uproar. But there were some Jews from Asia — who ought to have been present before you and to make accusation, if they should have anything against me. Or else let these men themselves tell what misdeed they found when I stood before the Council, other than for this one statement which I shouted out while standing among them, 'For the resurrection of the dead I am on trial before you today'" (Ac. 24:10-21).

IN THE BOOK OF ROMANS

In It the Righteousness of God Is Revealed from Faith to Faith

"For I am not ashamed of the gospel, for it is the power of God for salvation to everyone who believes, to the Jew first and also to the Greek. For in it the righteousness of God is revealed from faith to faith; as it is written, 'BUT THE

RIGHTEOUS man SHALL LIVE BY FAITH'" (Ro. 1:16-17).

The Day of Wrath and Revelation of the Righteous Judgment of God

"Therefore you have no excuse, everyone of you who passes judgment, for in that which you judge another, you condemn yourself; for you who judge practice the same things. And we know that the judgment of God rightly falls upon those who practice such things. But do you suppose this, O man, when you pass judgment on those who practice such things and do the same yourself, that you will escape the judgment of God? Or do you think lightly of the riches of His kindness and tolerance and patience, not knowing that the kindness of God leads you to repentance? But because of your stubbornness and unrepentant heart you are storing up wrath for yourself in the day of wrath and revelation of the righteous judgment of God, who WILL RENDER TO EACH PERSON ACCORDING TO HIS DEEDS: to those who by perseverance in doing good seek for glory and honor and immortality, eternal life; but to those who are selfishly ambitious and do not obey the truth, but obey unrighteousness, wrath and indignation. There will be tribulation and distress for every soul of man who does evil, of the Jew first and also of the Greek, but glory and honor and peace to everyone who does good, to the Jew first and also to the Greek. For there is no partiality with God" (Ro. 2:1-11).

A Righteous Man

"For while we were still helpless, at the right time Christ died for the ungodly. For one will hardly die for a righteous man; though perhaps for the good man someone would dare even to die. But God demonstrates His own love toward us, in that while we were yet sinners, Christ died for us. Much more then, having now been justified by His blood, we shall be saved from the wrath of God through Him. For if while we were enemies we were reconciled to God through the death of His Son, much more, having been reconciled, we shall be saved by His life. And not only this, but we also exult in God through our Lord Jesus Christ, through whom we have now received the reconciliation" (Ro. 5:6-11).

Through the Obedience of the One the Many Will Be Made Righteous

"So then as through one transgression there resulted condemnation to all men, even so through one act of righteousness there resulted justification of life to all men. For as through the one man's disobedience the many were made sinners, even so through the obedience of the One the many will be made righteous. The Law came in so that the transgression would increase; but where sin increased, grace abounded all the more, so that, as sin reigned in death, even so grace would reign through righteousness to eternal life through Jesus Christ our Lord" (Ro. 5:18-21).

The Commandment Is Holy and Righteous and Good

"What shall we say then? Is the Law sin? May it never be! On the contrary, I would not have come to know sin except through the Law; for I would not have known about coveting if the Law had not said, 'YOU SHALL NOT COVET.' But sin, taking opportunity through the commandment, produced in me coveting of every kind; for apart from the Law sin is dead. I was once alive apart from the Law; but when the commandment came, sin became alive and I died; and this commandment, which was to result in life, proved to result in death for me; for sin, taking an opportunity through the commandment, deceived me and through it killed me. So then, the Law is holy, and the commandment is holy and righteous and good" (Ro. 7:7-12).

IN THE BOOK OF GALATIANS

The Righteous Man Shall Live by Faith

"For as many as are of the works of the Law are under a curse; for it is written, 'CURSED IS EVERYONE WHO DOES NOT ABIDE BY ALL THINGS WRITTEN IN THE BOOK OF THE LAW,

TO PERFORM THEM.' Now that no one is justified by the Law before God is evident; for, 'THE RIGHTEOUS MAN SHALL LIVE BY FAITH.' However, the Law is not of faith; on the contrary, 'HE WHO PRACTICES THEM SHALL LIVE BY THEM.' Christ redeemed us from the curse of the Law, having become a curse for us — for it is written, 'CURSED IS EVERYONE WHO HANGS ON A TREE' — in order that in Christ Jesus the blessing of Abraham might come to the Gentiles, so that we would receive the promise of the Spirit through faith" (Gal. 3:10-14).

IN THE BOOK OF THESSALONIANS

God's Righteous Judgment

"We ought always to give thanks to God for you, brethren, as is only fitting, because your faith is greatly enlarged, and the love of each one of you toward one another grows ever greater; therefore, we ourselves speak proudly of you among the churches of God for your perseverance and faith in the midst of all your persecutions and afflictions which you endure. This is a plain indication of God's righteous judgment so that you will be considered worthy of the kingdom of God, for which indeed you are suffering. For after all it is only just for God to repay with affliction those who afflict you, and to give relief to you who are afflicted and to us as well when the Lord Jesus will be revealed from heaven with His mighty angels in flaming fire, dealing out retribution to those who do not know God and to those who do not obey the gospel of our Lord Jesus. These will pay the penalty of eternal destruction, away from the presence of the Lord and from the glory of His power, when He comes to be glorified in His saints on that day, and to be marveled at among all who have believed—for our testimony to you was believed. To this end also we pray for you always, that our God will count you worthy of your calling, and fulfill every desire for goodness and the work of faith with power, so that the name of our Lord Jesus will be glorified in you, and you in Him, according to the grace of our God and the Lord Jesus Christ" (2Th. 1:3-12).

IN THE BOOK OF 1 TIMOTHY

The Fact that Law Is Mot Made for a Righteous Person, but for Those Who Are Lawless

"But we know that the Law is good, if one uses it lawfully, realizing the fact that law is not made for a righteous person, but for those who are lawless and rebellious, for the ungodly and sinners, for the unholy and profane, for those who kill their fathers or mothers, for murderers and immoral men and homosexuals and kidnappers and liars and perjurers, and whatever else is contrary to sound teaching, according to the glorious gospel of the blessed God, with which I have been entrusted" (1Ti. 1:8-11).

IN THE BOOK OF 2 TIMOTHY

The Lord, the Righteous Judge, Will Award to Me on That Day

"For I am already being poured out as a drink offering, and the time of my departure has come. I have fought the good fight, I have finished the course, I have kept the faith; in the future there is laid up for me the crown of righteousness, which the Lord, the righteous Judge, will award to me on that day; and not only to me, but also to all who have loved His appearing" (2Ti. 4:6-8).

IN THE BOOK OF HEBREWS

The Righteous Scepter

"For to which of the angels did He ever say, 'YOU ARE MY SON, TODAY I HAVE BEGOTTEN YOU'? And again, 'I WILL BE A FATHER TO HIM AND HE SHALL BE A SON TO ME'? And when He again brings the firstborn into the world, He says, 'AND LET ALL THE ANGELS OF GOD WORSHIP HIM.' And of the angels He says, 'WHO MAKES HIS ANGELS WINDS, AND HIS MINISTERS A FLAME OF FIRE.' But of the Son He says, 'YOUR THRONE, O GOD, IS FOREVER AND EVER, AND THE RIGHTEOUS SCEPTER IS THE SCEPTER OF HIS

KINGDOM. YOU HAVE LOVED RIGHTEOUSNESS AND HATED LAWLESSNESS; THEREFORE GOD, YOUR GOD, HAS ANOINTED YOU WITH THE OIL OF GLADNESS ABOVE YOUR COMPANIONS.' And, 'YOU, LORD, IN THE BEGINNING LAID THE FOUNDATION OF THE EARTH, AND THE HEAVENS ARE THE WORKS OF YOUR HANDS; THEY WILL PERISH, BUT YOU REMAIN; AND THEY ALL WILL BECOME OLD LIKE A GARMENT, AND LIKE A MANTLE YOU WILL ROLL THEM UP; LIKE A GARMENT THEY WILL ALSO BE CHANGED. BUT YOU ARE THE SAME, AND YOUR YEARS WILL NOT COME TO AN END.' But to which of the angels has He ever said, 'SIT AT MY RIGHT HAND, UNTIL I MAKE YOUR ENEMIES A FOOTSTOOL FOR YOUR FEET'? Are they not all ministering spirits, sent out to render service for the sake of those who will inherit salvation" (Heb. 1:5-14)?

But My Righteous One Shall Live by Faith

"But remember the former days, when, after being enlightened, you endured a great conflict of sufferings, partly by being made a public spectacle through reproaches and tribulations, and partly by becoming sharers with those who were so treated. For you showed sympathy to the prisoners and accepted joyfully the seizure of your property, knowing that you have for yourselves a better possession and a lasting one. Therefore, do not throw away your confidence, which has a great reward. For you have need of endurance, so that when you have done the will of God, you may receive what was promised. FOR YET IN A VERY LITTLE WHILE, HE WHO IS COMING WILL COME, AND WILL NOT DELAY. BUT MY RIGHTEOUS ONE SHALL LIVE BY FAITH; AND IF HE SHRINKS BACK, MY SOUL HAS NO PLEASURE IN HIM. But we are not of those who shrink back to destruction, but of those who have faith to the preserving of the soul" (Heb. 10:32-39).

He Was Righteous

"By faith we understand that the worlds were prepared by the word of God, so that what is seen was not made out of things which are visible. By faith Abel offered to God a better sacrifice than Cain, through which he obtained the testimony that he was righteous, God testifying about his gifts, and through faith, though he is dead, he still speaks. By faith Enoch was taken up so that he would not see death; AND HE WAS NOT FOUND BECAUSE GOD TOOK HIM UP; for he obtained the witness that before his being taken up he was pleasing to God. And without faith it is impossible to please Him, for he who comes to God must believe that He is and that He is a rewarder of those who seek Him. By faith Noah, being warned by God about things not yet seen, in reverence prepared an ark for the salvation of his household, by which he condemned the world, and became an heir of the righteousness which is according to faith" (Heb. 11:3-7).

The Spirits of the Righteous

"For you have not come to a mountain that can be touched and to a blazing fire, and to darkness and gloom and whirlwind, and to the blast of a trumpet and the sound of words which sound was such that those who heard begged that no further word be spoken to them. For they could not bear the command, 'IF EVEN A BEAST TOUCHES THE MOUNTAIN, IT WILL BE STONED.' And so terrible was the sight, that Moses said, 'I AM FULL OF FEAR and trembling.' But you have come to Mount Zion and to the city of the living God, the heavenly Jerusalem, and to myriads of angels, to the general assembly and church of the firstborn who are enrolled in heaven, and to God, the Judge of all, and to the spirits of the righteous made perfect, and to Jesus, the mediator of a new covenant, and to the sprinkled blood, which speaks better than the blood of Abel" (Heb. 12:18-24).

IN THE BOOK OF JAMES

You Have Condemned and Put to Death the Righteous Man

"Come now, you rich, weep and howl for your miseries which are coming upon you. Your riches have rotted and your garments have become moth-eaten. Your gold and your silver have rusted; and their rust will be a witness against you and will consume your flesh like fire. It is in the last days that you have stored up your treasure! Behold, the pay of the laborers who mowed your fields, and which has been withheld by you, cries out against you; and the outcry of those who did the harvesting has reached the ears of the Lord of Sabaoth. You have lived luxuriously on the earth and led a life of wanton pleasure; you have fattened your hearts in a day of slaughter. You have condemned and put to death the righteous man; he does not resist you" (Jas. 5:1-6).

The Effective Prayer of a Righteous Man Can Accomplish Much

"Is anyone among you suffering? Then he must pray. Is anyone cheerful? He is to sing praises. Is anyone among you sick? Then he must call for the elders of the church and they are to pray over him, anointing him with oil in the name of the Lord; and the prayer offered in faith will restore the one who is sick, and the Lord will raise him up, and if he has committed sins, they will be forgiven him. Therefore, confess your sins to one another, and pray for one another so that you may be healed. The effective prayer of a righteous man can accomplish much. Elijah was a man with a nature like ours, and he prayed earnestly that it would not rain, and it did not rain on the earth for three years and six months. Then he prayed again, and the sky poured rain and the earth produced its fruit" (Jas. 5:13-18).

IN THE BOOK OF 1 PETER

For the Eyes of the Lord Are Toward the Righteous

"To sum up, all of you be harmonious, sympathetic, brotherly, kindhearted, and humble in spirit; not returning evil for evil or insult for insult, but giving a blessing instead; for you were called for the very purpose that you might inherit a blessing. For, 'THE ONE WHO DESIRES LIFE, TO LOVE AND SEE GOOD DAYS, MUST KEEP HIS TONGUE FROM EVIL AND HIS LIPS FROM SPEAKING DECEIT. HE MUST TURN AWAY FROM EVIL AND DO GOOD; HE MUST SEEK PEACE AND PURSUE IT. FOR THE EYES OF THE LORD ARE TOWARD THE RIGHTEOUS, AND HIS EARS ATTEND TO THEIR PRAYER, BUT THE FACE OF THE LORD IS AGAINST THOSE WHO DO EVIL'" (1Pe. 3:8-12).

Chapter Seven

The Righteous Is Saved

"Beloved, do not be surprised at the fiery ordeal among you, which comes upon you for your testing, as though some strange thing were happening to you; but to the degree that you share the sufferings of Christ, keep on rejoicing, so that also at the revelation of His glory you may rejoice with exultation. If you are reviled for the name of Christ, you are blessed, because the Spirit of glory and of God rests on you. Make sure that none of you suffers as a murderer, or thief, or evildoer, or a troublesome meddler; but if anyone suffers as a Christian, he is not to be ashamed, but is to glorify God in this name. For it is time for judgment to begin with the household of God; and if it begins with us first, what will be the outcome for those who do not obey the gospel of God? AND IF IT IS WITH DIFFICULTY THAT THE RIGHTEOUS IS SAVED, WHAT WILL BECOME OF THE GODLESS MAN AND THE SINNER? Therefore, those also who suffer according to the will of God shall entrust their souls to a faithful Creator in doing what is right" (1Pe. 4:12-19).

IN THE BOOK OF 2 PETER

He Rescued Righteous Lot

"For if God did not spare angels when they sinned, but cast them into hell and committed them to pits of darkness, reserved for judgment;

and did not spare the ancient world, but preserved Noah, a preacher of righteousness, with seven others, when He brought a flood upon the world of the ungodly; and if He condemned the cities of Sodom and Gomorrah to destruction by reducing them to ashes, having made them an example to those who would live ungodly lives thereafter; and if He rescued righteous Lot, oppressed by the sensual conduct of unprincipled men (for by what he saw and heard that righteous man, while living among them, felt his righteous soul tormented day after day by their lawless deeds), then the Lord knows how to rescue the godly from temptation, and to keep the unrighteous under punishment for the day of judgment, and especially those who indulge the flesh in its corrupt desires and despise authority" (2Pe. 2:4-10).

IN THE BOOK OF 1 JOHN

He Is Faithful and Righteous to Forgive Us Our Sins

"This is the message we have heard from Him and announce to you, that God is Light, and in Him there is no darkness at all. If we say that we have fellowship with Him and yet walk in the darkness, we lie and do not practice the truth; but if we walk in the Light as He Himself is in the Light, we have fellowship with one another, and the blood of Jesus His Son cleanses us from all sin. If we say that we have no sin, we are deceiving ourselves and the truth is not in us. If we confess our sins, He is faithful and righteous to forgive us our sins and to cleanse us from all unrighteousness. If we say that we have not sinned, we make Him a liar and His word is not in us" (1Jn. 1:5-10).

We Have an Advocate with the Father, Jesus Christ the Righteous

"My little children, I am writing these things to you so that you may not sin. And if anyone sins, we have an Advocate with the Father, Jesus Christ the righteous; and He Himself is the propitiation for our sins; and not for ours only, but also for those of the whole world" (1Jn. 2:1-2).

He Is Righteous

"Now, little children, abide in Him, so that when He appears, we may have confidence and not shrink away from Him in shame at His coming. If you know that He is righteous, you know that everyone also who practices righteousness is born of Him" (1Jn. 2:28-29).

The One Who Practices Righteousness Is Righteous

"Everyone who practices sin also practices lawlessness; and sin is lawlessness. You know that He appeared in order to take away sins; and in

Him there is no sin. No one who abides in Him sins; no one who sins has seen Him or knows Him. Little children, make sure no one deceives you; the one who practices righteousness is righteous, just as He is righteous; the one who practices sin is of the devil; for the devil has sinned from the beginning. The Son of God appeared for this purpose, to destroy the works of the devil. No one who is born of God practices sin, because His seed abides in him; and he cannot sin, because he is born of God. By this the children of God and the children of the devil are obvious: anyone who does not practice righteousness is not of God, nor the one who does not love his brother" (1Jn. 3:4-10).

His Deeds Were Evil, and His Brother's Were Righteous

"For this is the message which you have heard from the beginning, that we should love one another; not as Cain, who was of the evil one and slew his brother. And for what reason did he slay him? Because his deeds were evil, and his brother's were righteous" (1Jn. 3:11-12).

IN THE BOOK OF REVELATION

Righteous and True Are Your Ways

"And I saw something like a sea of glass mixed with fire, and those who had been victorious over the beast and his image and the number of his name, standing on the sea of glass, holding harps of God. And they sang the song of Moses, the bond-servant of God, and the song of the Lamb, saying, 'Great and marvelous are Your works, O Lord God, the Almighty; Righteous and true are Your ways, King of the nations! Who will not fear, O Lord, and glorify Your name? For You alone are holy; For ALL THE NATIONS WILL COME AND WORSHIP BEFORE YOU, FOR YOUR RIGHTEOUS ACTS HAVE BEEN REVEALED'" (Rev. 15:2-4).

Righteous Are You, Who Are and Who Were, O Holy One

"Then the third angel poured out his bowl into the rivers and the springs of waters; and they became blood. And I heard the angel of the waters saying, 'Righteous are You, who are and who were, O Holy One, because You judged these things; for they poured out the blood of saints and prophets, and You have given them blood to drink. They deserve it.' And I heard the altar saying, 'Yes, O Lord God, the Almighty, true and righteous are Your judgments'" (Rev. 16:4-7).

His Judgments Are True and Righteous

"After these things I heard something like a loud voice of a great multitude in heaven, saying, 'Hallelujah! Salvation and glory and power belong to our God; BECAUSE HIS JUDGMENTS ARE TRUE AND RIGHTEOUS; for He has judged the great harlot who was corrupting the earth with her immorality, and HE HAS AVENGED THE BLOOD OF HIS BOND-SERVANTS ON HER.' And a second time they said, 'Hallelujah! HER SMOKE RISES UP FOREVER AND EVER.' And the twenty-four elders and the four living creatures fell down and worshiped God who sits on the throne saying, 'Amen. Hallelujah'" (Rev. 19:1-4)!

The Fine Linen Is the Righteous Acts of the Saints

"And a voice came from the throne, saying, 'Give praise to our God, all you His bond-servants, you who fear Him, the small and the great.' Then I heard something like the voice of a great multitude and like the sound of many waters and like the sound of mighty peals of thunder, saying, 'Hallelujah! For the Lord our God, the Almighty, reigns. Let us rejoice and be glad and give the glory to Him, for the marriage of the Lamb has come and His bride has made herself ready.' It was given to her to clothe herself in fine linen, bright and clean; for the fine linen is the righteous acts of the saints" (Rev. 19:5-8).

Let the One Who Is Righteous, Still Practice Righteousness

"And he said to me, 'Do not seal up the words of the prophecy of this book, for the time is near. Let the one who does wrong, still do wrong; and the one who is filthy, still be filthy; and let the one who is righteous, still practice righteousness; and the one who is holy, still keep himself holy'" (Rev. 22:10-11).

DAILY FAITH CONFESSIONS

(These are not direct quotations from the Bible but are paraphrased confessions based on scripture.)
SAY THEM OUT LOUD.

I am God's child (Jn. 1:12). I am royalty (1 Pet. 2:9). I am hidden with Christ in God (Col. 3:3). I am united with the Lord (1 Cor. 6:17). I am a friend of Christ (Jn. 15:15). I am raised up with Him, and seated with Him in heavenly places in Christ Jesus (Eph. 2:6). I was bought with a price (1 Cor. 6:19-20). I am blessed when I come in, and blessed shall I be when I go out (Deut. 28:6). I am a personal witness of Christ (Acts 1:8). I am a saint who prays in the Holy Spirit to keep myself in the love of God (Jude 1:20-21). I draw near with confidence to the throne of grace (Heb. 4:16). I have been adopted by the Father (Eph. 1:5). I am the salt and light of the earth (Mt. 5:13). I am the head and not the tail, and I am above, and not underneath. I am the lender and not the borrower (Deut. 28:13). I have authority to trample serpents and scorpions and over all the power of the enemy (Lk. 10:19). I am a member of the body of Christ (1 Cor. 12:27). God blessed me to be fruitful, and multiply, and replenish the earth, and subdue it: and have dominion (Gen. 1:28). I cannot be separated from God's love (Ro. 8:39). The good work God has begun in me will be perfected (Phil. 1:5). I can do all things through Christ who strengthens me (Phil. 4:13). No weapon that is formed against me will prosper (Is. 54:17). So then faith cometh by hearing, and hearing by the word of God (Ro. 10:17 KJV). Faith is my currency to operate in the kingdom of God (Ro. 14:23). I am God's workmanship created in Christ Jesus for good works, which God prepared beforehand (Eph. 2:10). I have been appointed to bear fruit, and that my fruit would remain (Jn. 15:16). I am being wise when I am winning souls for King Jesus (Pr. 11:30). My body is the temple of the Holy Spirit (1 Cor. 6:19). I have access to God through the Holy Spirit (Eph. 2:18). I have been justified (Ro. 5:1). Therefore there is now no condemnation for those who are in Christ Jesus (Ro. 8:1). Greater is He who is in me than he who is in the world (1 Jn. 4:4). I will do greater works than Jesus because He went to the Father (Jn. 14:12). As God was with Moses, He will be with me; God will not fail me or forsake me (Jos. 1:5). I see myself the way God see me. God sees me as a king (Gen, 17:6, Rev. 1:6) God sees me as royalty (1 Pet. 2:9). God sees me as the righteousness of God in Christ, bold as a lion (Ro. 3:22, Pr. 28:1). God sees me without spot or wrinkle because of the blood of Jesus (1 Pet. 1:19). I am having faith for big things because God owns everything and I'm His son (Ps. 24:1). No man will be able to stand before me all the days of my life (Jos. 1:5). My Father is glorified by this that I bear much fruit, and proves I'm a disciple (see Jn. 15:8). I think big and confess big things because God is big (Ps. 24:1). I will respect God for the big God that He is and my mouth will create whatever I want (Lk. 6:45). I no longer think of millions, my renewed mind thinks of billions because the wealth of the wicked is laid up for the righteous (Pr. 13:22). The sinner's job is to gather and collect for the one who is good in God's sight (Ecc. 2:26). Redemption is not complete without prosperity. Jesus hung on the cross so I can have the whole package, not just salvation (2 Cor. 8:9). I don't have to qualify, Jesus has qualified me. Jesus reversed the curse. The devil is a liar, and Jesus is the Messiah. Jesus is made unto me wisdom, righteousness, sanctification, and redemption (1 Cor. 1:30). I submit to God, I resist the devil and he flees from me (Jas. 4:7). For God has not given me the spirit of fear; but of power, and of love, and of a sound mind (2 Tim. 1:7). The Holy Spirit will teach me all things (Jn. 14:26). The Holy Spirit will guide me into all truth (Jn.16:13). The Holy Spirit abides in me, and I don't need anyone to teach me, but the anointing teaches me all things (1 Jn. 2:27). I quench fiery darts from the wicked one with the shield of faith (Eph. 6:16). I stand firm against the schemes of the devil (Eph. 6:11). I already have the victory and Satan cannot back me up. I advance and hold. Advance and hold to victory after victory (2 Cor. 2:14). I walk in love and live by faith (Gal. 5:6). I have been redeemed from the curse of the law, poverty, sickness, and spiritual death (Gal. 3:13; Deut. 28). I bear much fruit. I'm God's workmanship created beforehand for good works (Eph. 2:10). God's favor is on my life (Ps. 3:8). God blesses me and His favor surrounds me as with a shield (Ps. 5:12). The kingdom of God is within me (Lk. 17:21). I have a production plant inside of me that bears fruit to change the world (Gen. 1:28). God gives me power to get wealth to establish His covenant on earth (Deut. 8:18). I am blessed to be a blessing (Gen. 12:2). I have Satan on the run and will make a mockery of him (Jas. 4:7). No man will be able to stand before me all the days of my life (Jos. 1:5). God's angels keep me in all my ways (Ps. 91: 11).

PRAYER FOR SALVATION

Say the following prayer out loud.

Heavenly Father, I am a sinner and I need a Savior. I confess Jesus Christ as the Lord of my life. I repent of all my sins. Father, I truly believe you raised Jesus from the dead. I pray this prayer in Jesus' name. Father, I am your child because Jesus is my Lord. I want to receive the fullness of the Holy Spirit. Holy Spirit come into me and fill me so I can be a mighty witness for King Jesus. I pray this prayer in Jesus' name. Amen.

PRAYER FOR BAPTISM OF THE HOLY SPIRIT

Say the following prayer out loud.

Father, I am your child because Jesus is my Lord. Jesus said, "How much more shall your heavenly Father give the Holy Spirit to those who ask Him." I ask you now in the name of Jesus to fill me with the Holy Spirit. Thank you, Father, I received the baptism of the Holy Spirit by faith. I yield my vocal organs and expect to speak in tongues as the Holy Spirit gives me utterance in Jesus name. Father, I plan to pray in the Holy Spirit building myself up on my most holy faith, and keep myself in the love of God, as mentioned in Jude 20 and 21. In Jesus name I decree it. Amen.

ABOUT THE AUTHOR

Eugene Carvalho is an administrator, Christian author of seventy-seven books, and the founder of Receiving by Faith. God uses him in the offices of pastor, evangelist and prophet. He holds a bachelor's degree in biblical studies and a double minor in pastoral ministry and world missions. He also holds a master's degree in practical theology. Eugene prayed for a translator and God sent his wife Mercedes who has a six-year degree in Spanish from a university in Tampico, Mexico. They have participated in evangelism in the streets of Mexico for many years. They have also traveled to churches all over the United States and the nation of Mexico winning souls and preaching the gospel of the kingdom. Their website for their ministry is: www.receivingbyfaith.org.

BOOKS BY EUGENE IN ENGLISH

For a complete list of other books by Eugene visit receivingbyfaith.org or amazon.com.

Receiving by Faith
Faith for Every Day: 365 Daily Devotions
Faith Cometh by Hearing, and Hearing by the Word of God
Faith, Hope, and Love
Walk in Love and Live by Faith
Topical Christian Handbook and Scripture Guide
The Gospel Is the Power of God unto Salvation
Seed Time and Harvest Time
Your New Identity in Christ
The Cross and the Blood
The Holy Spirit
The Attributes of God
The Favor of God
The Glory of God
The Grace of God
The Power of God
The Promises of God
The Throne of God
The Holy Spirit Will Guide You into All Truth
The New Testament Church: A Survey from the Book of Ephesians
Vengeance and Recompense
God's Angel's
Prayer and Fasting
God's Mighty Prophets
A Survey of Jesus Through the Epistles

You Have Authority and Power: Take Back What the Devil Stole

Be Strong and Courageous

Prayer and Praise: The Big Artillery

Apostles and Prophets: The Foundation of the Church

Covenant: A Concise Survey

Sow Then Reap a Harvest

God Has Not Given Us a Spirit of Timidity, But of Power, Love, and Discipline

Blessed and Highly Favored

Grace and Peace Be Multiplied Unto You

Your Word Is a Lamp to Me Feet

John: A Key Word Study Made Simple

For Momentary, Light Affliction Is Producing For Us an Eternal Weight of Glory

Prayer Is Powerful: What the Bible Has to Say

My People Are Destroyed By Lack of Knowledge

God Deserves Pure Worship

The Mouth of the Righteous is a Fountain of Life

The Lord Requires Integrity: The Major Element of Leadership

Weeping May Last for the Night, But a Shout of Joy Comes in the Morning

A Topical Look at the Book of Deuteronomy

A Topical Look at the Book of Psalms

A Topical Look at the Book of Proverbs

A Topical Look at the Book of Isaiah

A Topical Look at the Book of John

A Topical Look at the Book of Hebrews

A Topical Look at the Book of Revelation

BOOKS BY EUGENE IN SPANISH

Las Promesas de Dios
Los Salmos de David
Lo Sobrenatural: Lo que la Bíblia Tiene que Decir
Una Mirada Topica Del Libro De Los Salmos
Dios es Amor: Lo que la Biblia Tiene que Decir
La Adquisición de la Sabiduría es Vital: Lo que la
Biblia Tiene que Decir

NOTES

<u>NOTES</u>

214

<u>NOTES</u>

215

www.ingramcontent.com/pod-product-compliance
Lightning Source LLC
Chambersburg PA
CBHW071411150726
48000CB00001B/269